ATLAS OF THE
CONSTELLATIONS

ATLAS OF THE
CONSTELLATIONS

KNOW YOUR WAY AROUND THE NIGHT SKY

GILES SPARROW

amber
BOOKS

First published in 2007 by
Amber Books Ltd
Bradley's Close
74–77 White Lion Street
London N1 9PF
United Kingdom
www.amberbooks.co.uk

Copyright © Amber Books Ltd 2007

Reprinted in 2008

ISBN-13: 978-1-904687-75-7

Distributed in the UK by
Bookmart Ltd
Blaby Road
Wigston
Leicester LE18 4SE

Project Editor: James Bennett
Copy Editor: Constance Novis
Design: Joe Conneally

Printed in Dubai

Picture Credits
All images copyright Amber Books except for the following:
International Masters Publishers: 5, 9, 10 (bottom left), 102–107
Corbis/Roger Ressmeyer: 6
NASA: 10, 11, 12

Introducing the Night Sky

On a clear dark night, the sky seems to be filled with countless stars – far too many, you might think, for anyone to find them all, let alone know their patterns. But the task is not as daunting as it seems. Even in perfect viewing conditions, in reality, most people will only see about 2500 to 3000 stars, on average. This is still a great many, but it's surprisingly easy to learn your way around the sky using the constellations – and that's what this book will show you how to do.

When prehistoric astronomers first looked up at the sky, they made patterns out of the stars and told stories of the figures they saw there. The earliest legends are lost to us because people were studying the stars long before they were writing things down. However, from the time of ancient Babylon (before 1000 BC), there are written, carved and painted records of these patterns – the earliest constellations.

Asterisms

In its simplest form, a constellation is just a 'stick figure' made by joining up stars in the sky. Such patterns are also called 'asterisms'. All of today's constellations contain an asterism of some shape, and while astronomers generally agree which stars make up the asterism, they may not agree about precisely how they join up (in today's era of computer-controlled giant telescopes, professional astronomers generally leave asterisms to the amateurs). Some famous asterisms stretch across constellations (for example, the 'Summer Triangle' composed of the bright stars Vega, Deneb and Altair), and others are just smaller parts of a larger asterism (for example, the Square of Pegasus in Pegasus).

Classical constellations

Ancient civilizations all had their own constellations. These were normally closely associated with their culture and mythology, but there were often close parallels, sometimes because certain areas of sky objectively look like particular figures, and sometimes through cultural links. Claudius Ptolemaeus, or Ptolemy, an influential Egyptian-Greek astronomer who summed up much of classical astronomy in a book, the *Almagest*, drew up the definitive list of ancient constellations in the second century AD. Ptolemy's list included 48 constellations in all.

The Constellation of Orion

This long-exposure photograph shows the bright stars of Orion, including Betelgeuse and Rigel (see page 73). The brightest star, Sirius (far left), is in the constellation of Canis Major. At the bottom of the picture, the image has also captured the movement of a satellite.

For almost 1500 years, no one saw the need to adjust or add to Ptolemy's work, but all that changed in the sixteenth century. As European explorers journeyed into the southern hemisphere for the first time, they saw stars that were never visible from Ptolemy's Mediterranean latitudes, and they naturally formed their own constellations from them. Just as importantly, the invention of the telescope and the acceptance for the first time that Earth was not in the very middle of the Universe (and the stars were distant suns like our own) kicked the science of astronomy into a higher gear. If all the stars – not just the few really bright, named ones – were worth studying as objects in their own right, then astronomers needed new ways of identifying them individually. And more subdivisions – more constellations – helped that.

One result of this was an astronomical 'free for all'. Many observers invented new constellations in formerly uncharted areas of the sky, or even broke old constellations apart and plundered their stars, in a bid for textbook immortality. Many of the new constellations dating from this era were small and faint, and few of them resemble the objects for which they are named. Even as star atlases became more important, they were increasingly contradictory and inconsistent.

Cataloguing and naming the stars

Counterbalancing this increasing chaos in the heavens, the invention of the telescope also more or less coincided with the first serious attempts to systematically catalogue the individual stars. In his *Uranometria* of 1603, German astronomer Johannes Bayer introduced a new naming system for stars, using Greek letters (*see box*).

Bayer's idea was simple and ingenious. However, the lettering of the stars today is chaotic in places, thanks to a number of historical factors. For one thing, there was no consistent agreement on how far the constellations extended beyond their asterisms. For another, some of Bayer's constellations are no longer recognized, and some stars have swapped constellations. And on top of that, Bayer and those who followed in his footsteps seem to have made more than a few mistakes.

Nevertheless, Bayer's letters have stuck, mistakes and all, and no one has risked the confusion that would result from a wholesale relettering of the sky. Rather than recycle old catalogue systems, astronomers have preferred to pile new ones on top. As a result, most bright stars have quite a number of different catalogue names and numbers – none of which need worry us here, because this book is mostly concerned with the brightest stars.

Definitive list of constellations

Although the frenzy for inventing new constellations died away in the nineteenth century (perhaps because astronomers found a new source of immortality by discovering asteroids) some areas of the sky were still an inconsistent mess. And as telescopes grew ever more powerful and new objects were discovered, the question of which constellation they belonged to constantly returned. Finally, in 1929, the International Astronomical Union (IAU), the governing body of world astronomy, decided to set matters straight. They drew up a definitive list of 88 constellations (Ptolemy's 48, with 40 later additions), and redefined them as areas of sky with precise boundaries, not simply vague patterns of stars. Today's constellations fit together like a jigsaw puzzle, covering the entire sky so that every celestial object can be assigned to a constellation purely on the basis of its coordinates.

The celestial sphere

The constellations visible in your night sky depend on the time of year and your location on the surface of the Earth. It often helps to think about the sky as a 'celestial sphere', with the constellations attached to it, rotating around the Earth once a day (even though we've known this is a false picture since the sixteenth century).

In Bayer's system, the brightest star in each constellation was given the first letter of the Greek alphabet (Alpha, written α), the next brightest the second letter (Beta, written β) and so on. In this way, Bayer could consistently name the brightest 24 stars in each constellation.

UC	lc	Name	UC	lc	Name
A	α	alpha	N	ν	nu
B	β	beta	Ξ	ξ	xi
Γ	γ	gamma	O	o	omicron
Δ	δ	delta	Π	π	pi
E	ε	epsilon	P	ρ	rho
Z	ζ	zeta	Σ	σ	sigma
H	η	eta	T	τ	tau
Θ	θ	theta	Y	υ	upsilon
I	ι	iota	Φ	φ	phi
K	κ	kappa	X	χ	chi
Λ	λ	lambda	Ψ	ψ	psi
M	μ	mu	Ω	ω	omega

UC = UPPER CASE   lc = lower case

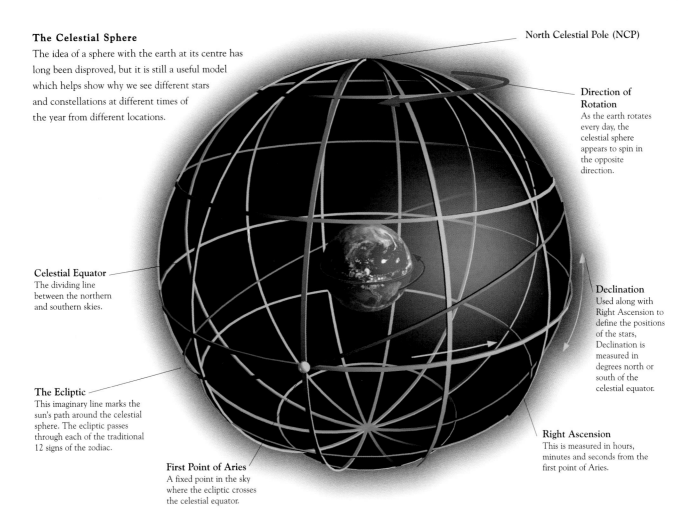

The Celestial Sphere
The idea of a sphere with the earth at its centre has long been disproved, but it is still a useful model which helps show why we see different stars and constellations at different times of the year from different locations.

North Celestial Pole (NCP)

Direction of Rotation
As the earth rotates every day, the celestial sphere appears to spin in the opposite direction.

Celestial Equator
The dividing line between the northern and southern skies.

Declination
Used along with Right Ascension to define the positions of the stars, Declination is measured in degrees north or south of the celestial equator.

The Ecliptic
This imaginary line marks the sun's path around the celestial sphere. The ecliptic passes through each of the traditional 12 signs of the zodiac.

First Point of Aries
A fixed point in the sky where the ecliptic crosses the celestial equator.

Right Ascension
This is measured in hours, minutes and seconds from the first point of Aries.

At any time, the Earth's surface blocks out our view of one half of the celestial sphere. The precise area we can see depends on which direction our part of the Earth is pointing. At the North Pole, we would be 'pointing' straight upwards, and could see the entire northern half of the sky, but none of the southern hemisphere stars. As the Earth rotated, the sky would seem to spin around the point directly above our head – the North Celestial Pole (NCP), marked by Polaris, the 'pole star' in Ursa Minor. For latitudes further to the south, Polaris is not directly overhead. It sinks lower in the sky, until at the equator, it sits directly on the horizon, but it always lies due north in the sky. As the NCP sinks lower towards the north, the celestial equator (the dividing line between the northern and southern skies) rises higher in the south, and more of the southern sky becomes visible. For example, at latitude 50°N, Polaris sits due north in the sky, at an angle of exactly 50° up from the horizon. The

celestial equator reaches a maximum altitude of 40° as it crosses the 'meridian' (the line joining north and south), due south and opposite the pole star, and as a result, stars as much as 40° south of the celestial equator can briefly be seen peaking above the southern horizon. At the equator, where the NCP lies exactly on the northern horizon and the South Celestial Pole (SCP) lies exactly on the southern horizon, the celestial equator is directly overhead and the entire sky wheels overhead in the course of 24 hours. In the southern hemisphere, the situation is exactly reversed, with the SCP due south in the sky, and the celestial equator reaching its maximum altitude due north.

Path of the Ecliptic
The other major factor that affects the visibility of constellations is the time of year. As the Earth orbits the Sun in the course of a year, and our point of view changes, the Sun appears to move

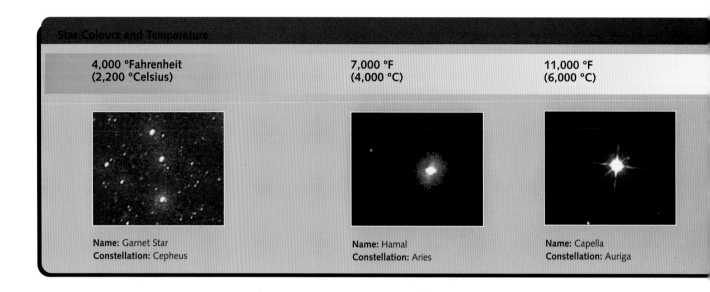

Star Colours and Temperature

4,000 °Fahrenheit (2,200 °Celsius)	7,000 °F (4,000 °C)	11,000 °F (6,000 °C)

Name: Garnet Star
Constellation: Cepheus

Name: Hamal
Constellation: Aries

Name: Capella
Constellation: Auriga

The Magnitude Scale

This chart shows the brightness of various celestial objects. Magnitude 6.0 is roughly the limit of visibility for the unaided human eye. The ancient Greeks were the first to use the magnitude scale, defining the brightest stars as 'first magnitude' and those on the limit of visibility as sixth magnitude. After its inclusion in Ptolemy's *Almagest*, this system was adopted unchanged through the middle ages. When the Renaissance astronomer Galileo discovered stars fainter than those which could be seen with the naked eye, he categorized the brightest as 'seventh magnitude'. Today's system, encompassing magnitudes from -30 to +30, was first formalized by English astronomer Norman Pogson (1829–1891), who defined that a difference of five magnitudes should equal a hundred-fold difference in brightness. In this way, the scale can embrace huge differences in brightness.

along a path called the ecliptic, which passes through the twelve constellations of the zodiac. Because our clock and calendar are built around the movement of the Sun rather than the stars, the sky gradually 'slips' in relation to the Sun, so that the constellations rise and set at different times. In general, constellations rise earlier through the year. For a couple of months, when they rise and set at the same time as the Sun, they may not be visible at all. Six months later, when they rise and set opposite the Sun, they will be visible all night long.

The ecliptic is not just important because of the movement of the Sun. It is also a projection of Earth's own orbit onto the sky, and because the planets all orbit in more or less the same plane, this is where the planets also spend the majority of the time. The ecliptic even provides the basis for measuring the positions of

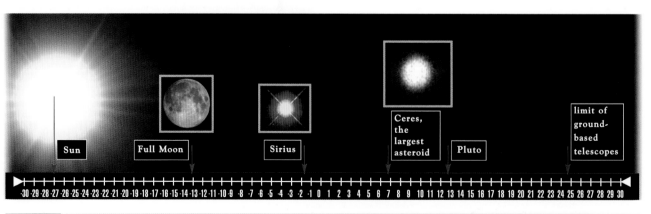

Sun Full Moon Sirius Ceres, the largest asteroid Pluto limit of ground-based telescopes

-30 -29 -28 -27 -26 -25 -24 -23 -22 -21 -20 -19 -18 -17 -16 -15 -14 -13 -12 -11 -10 -9 -8 -7 -6 -5 -4 -3 -2 -1 0 1 2 3 4 5 6 7 8 9 10 11 12 13 14 15 16 17 18 19 20 21 22 23 24 25 26 27 28 29 30

BRIGHTER

DIMMER

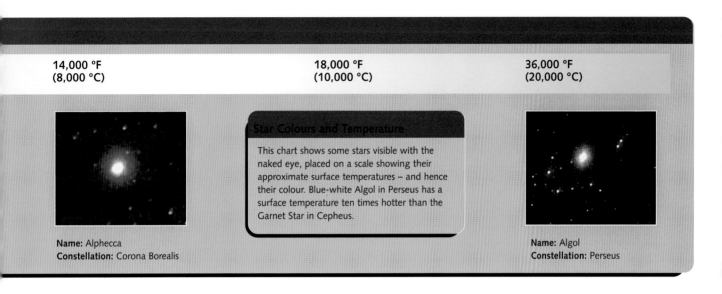

| 14,000 °F (8,000 °C) | 18,000 °F (10,000 °C) | 36,000 °F (20,000 °C) |

Star Colours and Temperature

This chart shows some stars visible with the naked eye, placed on a scale showing their approximate surface temperatures – and hence their colour. Blue-white Algol in Perseus has a surface temperature ten times hotter than the Garnet Star in Cepheus.

Name: Alphecca
Constellation: Corona Borealis

Name: Algol
Constellation: Perseus

stars. Astronomers measure a star's position in terms of its declination (angle from 0° to 90° north or south of the celestial equator), and its 'right ascension' (the time by which it 'lags behind' a fixed point in the sky called the first point of Aries, the crossing point of the ecliptic and the celestial equator), measured in hours, minutes and seconds from 0 to 24 hours.

All this can sound very complicated to a beginner, but don't worry – you don't need to understand it straight away in order to enjoy the rest of the book!

Objects in the night sky

The stars in the sky might all look the same at a casual glance, but this is far from the truth. The night sky is full of wonders. Along with the stars, there are star clusters and clouds, vast clumps of glowing gas and dark dust, and even galaxies beyond our own Milky Way.

A star's brightness in the sky is generally measured by a system called 'magnitude'. The lower a star's magnitude, the brighter it is. A difference in magnitude of 5 corresponds to a difference in brightness by a factor of 100. The faintest naked-eye stars are around magnitude 6.0, and the brightest stars in the sky have magnitudes below zero (Sirius, the brightest of all, is magnitude –1.4). Astronomers call the magnitude of objects as seen from Earth 'apparent magnitude', to distinguish from 'absolute magnitude', which is a measure of the star's true brilliance. However, here in this book, we make comparisons in terms of luminosity, which is defined as a star's total energy output compared to the Sun.

Using a variety of techniques, astronomers have measured the distance to many of these stars, and shown that there is no link between a star's distance and its apparent magnitude. In other words, some faint stars are nearby, while some bright ones are very far away. This means that there is even more variation in their real luminosity than there is in their apparent magnitude. The distances to stars are generally measured in light years. A light year serves as a conveniently huge astronomical measurement – the distance travelled by light in a year – equivalent to 5.9 million million miles (9.5 trillion kilometres).

Colour and temperature

Appearance can also reveal a lot about a star's nature. Red stars, for example, have comparatively cool surfaces (around 2,760°C/5000°F), while blue stars have much hotter surfaces (around 11,100°C/20,000°F). Because the star's surface temperature depends on the amount of energy pouring out of each square foot of its surface, stars with lower luminosity tend to be cooler and redder, while brighter stars tend to be hotter, white, or blue. Bright stars with comparatively cool yellow, orange, or red surfaces must be huge in order to stay so cool, and this has earned them the name 'giants'.

We now know that all stars pass through a giant phase towards the end of their lives, as they start to run out of fuel. Comparatively low-mass stars like the Sun then puff off their outer layers in a shell called a planetary nebula, leaving only a white dwarf, the name for the slowly cooling remains of their core. Stars more than eight times heavier than the Sun destroy themselves in huge supernova, creating a widely scattered cloud of gas called a supernova remnant. This leaves behind a superdense collapsed core, known as a neutron star or, in extreme cases, a black hole.

Clusters and nebulae

All the stars in the sky, and most of the other objects, are part of our huge spiral star system, the Milky Way galaxy. The galaxy contains around 200 billion stars, mixed with gas and dust. Amateur astronomers often refer to all the celestial objects that are not strictly stars as 'deep-sky' objects. Stars are born in loose clusters called 'open clusters', which often heat the gas around them so much that it glows, creating an 'emission nebula'. The gas can also shine by reflected light, and this is known as a 'reflection nebula'. Earlier in our galaxy's history, some stars formed huge dense clusters of many tens of thousands of red and yellow stars, called 'globular clusters'. These now orbit around the body of the galaxy. Because the Solar System sits inside the plane of the galaxy, we see it as the familiar trail of the Milky Way – a band that wraps all the way around the sky. This band is scattered with stars, clusters and the remnants of old dead stars – planetary nebulae formed by dying sun-like stars, and supernova remnants created in the spectacular and violent deaths of much heavier stars.

Beyond the limits of our galaxy lies a vast gulf of largely empty space. The Milky Way is orbited by smaller satellite galaxies, of which the most famous are the Magellanic Clouds of Tucana and Dorado, both more than 150,000 light years away. Nearest to us is the great Andromeda galaxy, 2.5 million light years away, and beyond this lie countless other galaxies – as numerous as the stars in the Milky Way – to the very limits of the Universe.

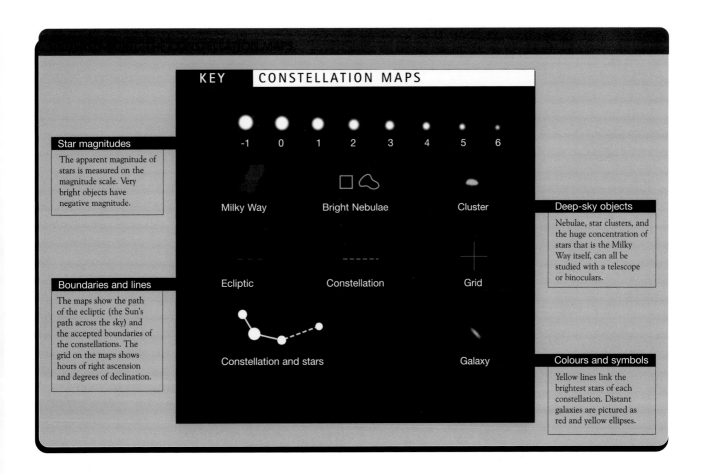

KEY   **CONSTELLATION MAPS**

-1   0   1   2   3   4   5   6

Milky Way   Bright Nebulae   Cluster

Ecliptic   Constellation   Grid

Constellation and stars   Galaxy

Star magnitudes

The apparent magnitude of stars is measured on the magnitude scale. Very bright objects have negative magnitude.

Boundaries and lines

The maps show the path of the ecliptic (the Sun's path across the sky) and the accepted boundaries of the constellations. The grid on the maps shows hours of right ascension and degrees of declination.

Deep-sky objects

Nebulae, star clusters, and the huge concentration of stars that is the Milky Way itself, can all be studied with a telescope or binoculars.

Colours and symbols

Yellow lines link the brightest stars of each constellation. Distant galaxies are pictured as red and yellow ellipses.

Orion Nebula

The photograph opposite, captured by the Hubble Space Telescope, shows more than 3000 individual stars in the region known as the Orion Nebula.

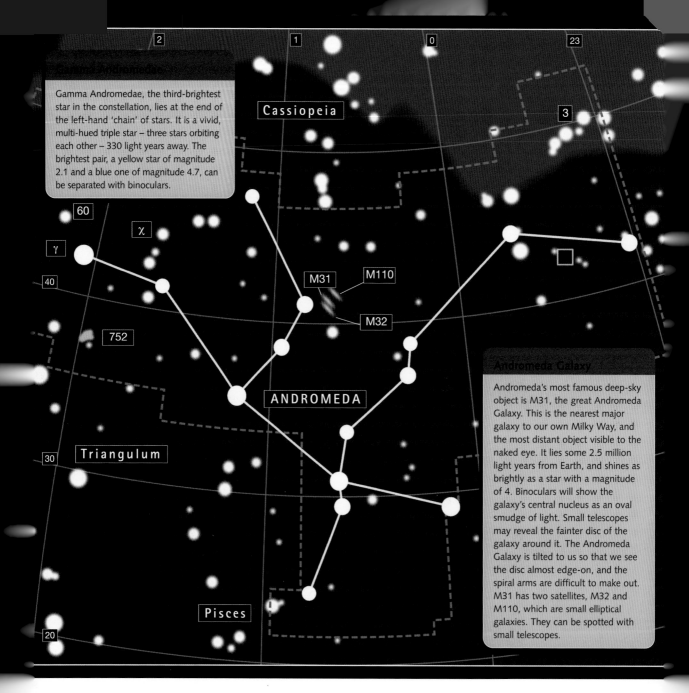

Gamma Andromedae

Gamma Andromedae, the third-brightest star in the constellation, lies at the end of the left-hand 'chain' of stars. It is a vivid, multi-hued triple star – three stars orbiting each other – 330 light years away. The brightest pair, a yellow star of magnitude 2.1 and a blue one of magnitude 4.7, can be separated with binoculars.

Cassiopeia

ANDROMEDA

Triangulum

Pisces

M31

M110

M32

Andromeda Galaxy

Andromeda's most famous deep-sky object is M31, the great Andromeda Galaxy. This is the nearest major galaxy to our own Milky Way, and the most distant object visible to the naked eye. It lies some 2.5 million light years from Earth, and shines as brightly as a star with a magnitude of 4. Binoculars will show the galaxy's central nucleus as an oval smudge of light. Small telescopes may reveal the fainter disc of the galaxy around it. The Andromeda Galaxy is tilted to us so that we see the disc almost edge-on, and the spiral arms are difficult to make out. M31 has two satellites, M32 and M110, which are small elliptical galaxies. They can be spotted with small telescopes.

Andromeda is one of the most famous of all the constellations. Even though none of the stars is very bright, it is still relatively easy to spot. Andromeda represents the chained princess rescued by the Greek hero, Perseus, and common names for the constellation include 'The Princess' and 'The Chained Maiden'. The brightest stars of the constellation form two distinct chains. These lead away from Alpha Andromedae, one of the most attractive double stars in the night sky. It looks like a single star to the naked eye but is actually a blue-white star of magnitude 2.1, 97 light years away.

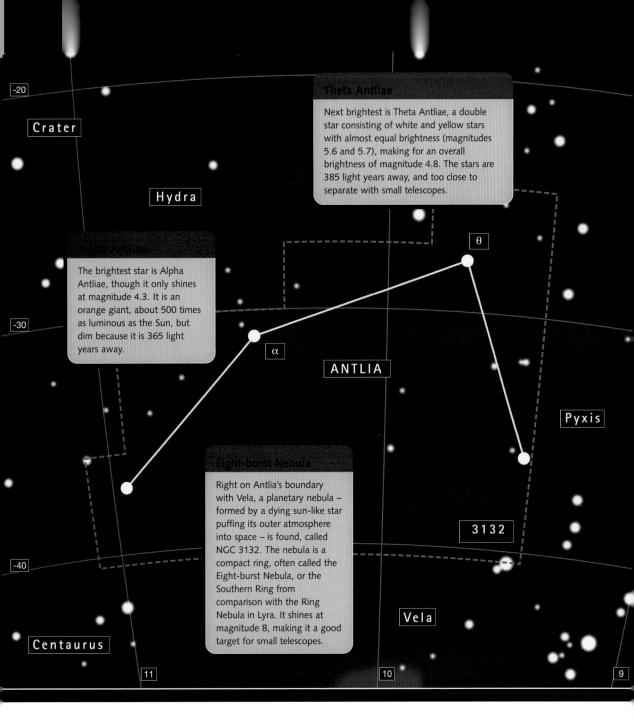

Theta Antliae

Next brightest is Theta Antliae, a double star consisting of white and yellow stars with almost equal brightness (magnitudes 5.6 and 5.7), making for an overall brightness of magnitude 4.8. The stars are 385 light years away, and too close to separate with small telescopes.

θ

Alpha Antliae

The brightest star is Alpha Antliae, though it only shines at magnitude 4.3. It is an orange giant, about 500 times as luminous as the Sun, but dim because it is 365 light years away.

α

ANTLIA

Pyxis

Eight-burst Nebula

Right on Antlia's boundary with Vela, a planetary nebula – formed by a dying sun-like star puffing its outer atmosphere into space – is found, called NGC 3132. The nebula is a compact ring, often called the Eight-burst Nebula, or the Southern Ring from comparison with the Ring Nebula in Lyra. It shines at magnitude 8, making it a good target for small telescopes.

3132

Vela

Centaurus

Crater

Hydra

-20

-30

-40

11

10

9

Antlia is one of many faint constellations introduced to the sky by French astronomer Nicolas Louis de Lacaille in the eighteenth century. Working in Cape Town, South Africa, he was one of the first astronomers to comprehensively study the southern skies. He named most of his constellations after scientific instruments, in this case the air or vacuum pump, invented by French scientist Denis Papin and British physicist Robert Boyle.

Antlia's stars are all faint. It sits in an empty region of sky north of the brighter stars in Vela, and south of the long, straggling constellation Hydra.

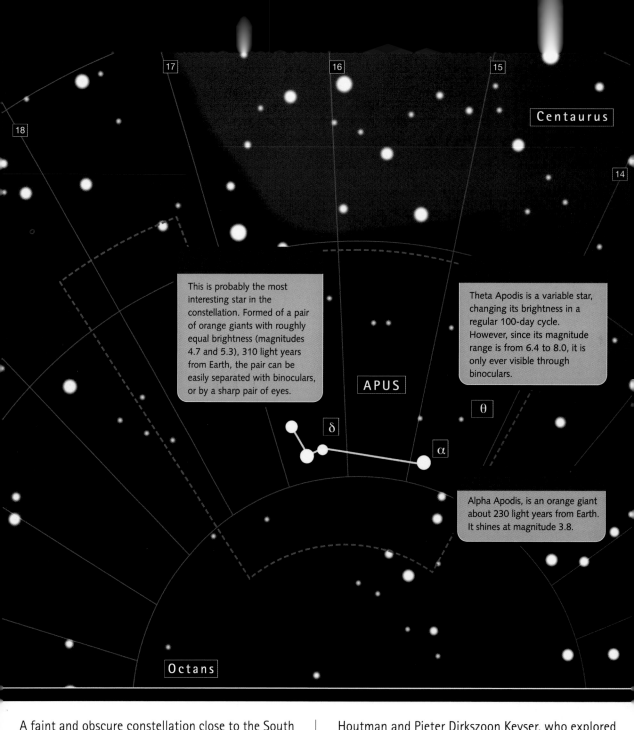

17
16
15

Centaurus

18

14

This is probably the most interesting star in the constellation. Formed of a pair of orange giants with roughly equal brightness (magnitudes 4.7 and 5.3), 310 light years from Earth, the pair can be easily separated with binoculars, or by a sharp pair of eyes.

Theta Apodis is a variable star, changing its brightness in a regular 100-day cycle. However, since its magnitude range is from 6.4 to 8.0, it is only ever visible through binoculars.

APUS

θ

δ

α

Alpha Apodis, is an orange giant about 230 light years from Earth. It shines at magnitude 3.8.

Octans

A faint and obscure constellation close to the South Celestial Pole and south of Centaurus, Apus is permanently visible from nearly the entire southern hemisphere. It has few objects of interest, however, and is difficult to identify. The pattern of faint stars was invented by Dutch explorers Frederick de Houtman and Pieter Dirkszoon Keyser, who explored the southern hemisphere in the 1590s. They named the constellation after the birds of paradise they saw on the island of New Guinea.

Apus lies just to the south of the Milky Way, in the barren area of sky around the South Celestial Pole.

Aquarius

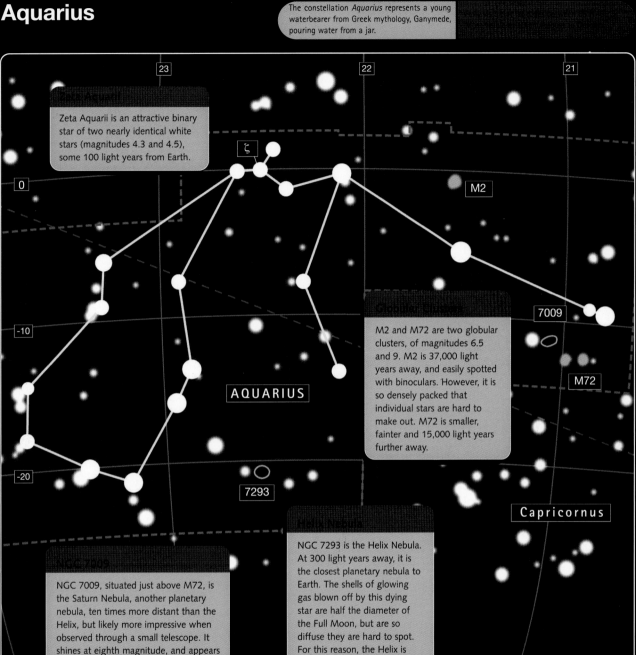

Zeta Aquarii

Zeta Aquarii is an attractive binary star of two nearly identical white stars (magnitudes 4.3 and 4.5), some 100 light years from Earth.

Globular Clusters

M2 and M72 are two globular clusters, of magnitudes 6.5 and 9. M2 is 37,000 light years away, and easily spotted with binoculars. However, it is so densely packed that individual stars are hard to make out. M72 is smaller, fainter and 15,000 light years further away.

NGC 7009

NGC 7009, situated just above M72, is the Saturn Nebula, another planetary nebula, ten times more distant than the Helix, but likely more impressive when observed through a small telescope. It shines at eighth magnitude, and appears as a compact turquoise ellipse.

Helix Nebula

NGC 7293 is the Helix Nebula. At 300 light years away, it is the closest planetary nebula to Earth. The shells of glowing gas blown off by this dying star are half the diameter of the Full Moon, but are so diffuse they are hard to spot. For this reason, the Helix is best seen through binoculars.

The constellation of Aquarius, though very famous, is in fact one of the fainter zodiac constellations. However, it is relatively easy to locate by spotting the Y-shaped group of stars known as the Water Jar just to its east. The constellation was seen as a figure pouring water from a jug as far back as ancient Babylonian times (before 1000 BC). It was the Greeks who identified the figure as the beautiful young boy, Ganymede. Zeus, king of the gods, fell in love with him and turned himself into an eagle (*see* Aquila, page 18) in order to carry Ganymede to Mount Olympus to be cup-bearer to the gods.

Aquila

Aquila is Latin for eagle, but this constellation is sometimes also called the vulture, from the Roman name for the grouping, *Vultur volans*.

21 **20** **19**

+20

Hercules

Alshain and Tarazed

Beta and Gamma Aquilae are yellow stars whose Bayer letters are the wrong way round. Tarazed (Gamma) is the brighter star, with a magnitude of 2.7, compared to Alshain's magnitude of 3.7. Tarazed is also much more distant, being a giant star 270 light years away, while Alshain is just 49 light years away.

γ

+10

Altair

AQUILA

6709

Altair is a nearby white star, just 17 light years from Earth. It shines at magnitude 0.8, and marks the southern tip of the 'Summer Triangle'. This is a distinctive pattern of stars in northern hemisphere summer skies, which also includes Deneb in Cygnus, and Vega in Lyra.

β

69

12

-10

Scutum

Aquila is one of 19 constellations catalogued by Ptolemy. Lying to the north of Sagittarius, and crossed by the Milky Way, Aquila lies on the celestial equator. The Greeks identified the constellation as the god Zeus, transformed into an eagle to abduct Ganymede (represented by nearby Aquarius, see page 17). It lies in the same direction as the Milky Way's central regions, so Aquila has many dense star fields towards the border with Scutum. The beginnings of the Cygnus Rift (a dark gap in the Milky Way caused by an intervening dust cloud) pass through Aquila.

Ara

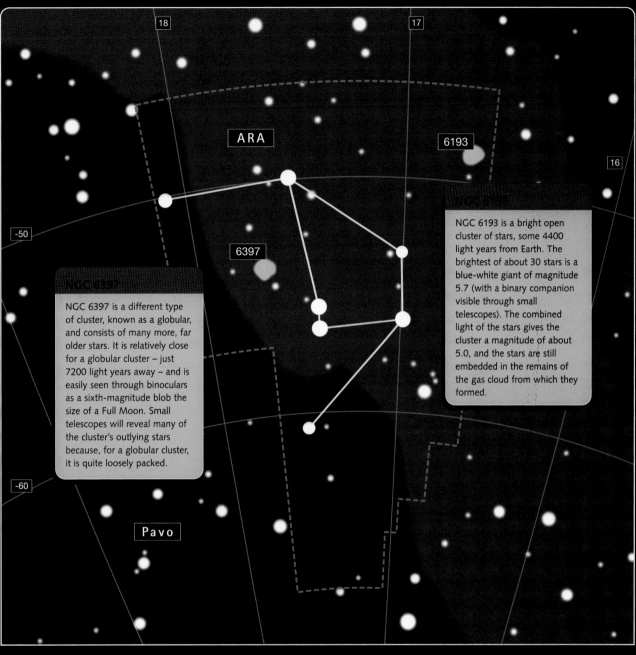

Ara is named after the altar on which the Greek gods swore an oath before struggling with the Titans for control of the universe.

ARA

6193

NGC 6193

NGC 6193 is a bright open cluster of stars, some 4400 light years from Earth. The brightest of about 30 stars is a blue-white giant of magnitude 5.7 (with a binary companion visible through small telescopes). The combined light of the stars gives the cluster a magnitude of about 5.0, and the stars are still embedded in the remains of the gas cloud from which they formed.

6397

NGC 6397

NGC 6397 is a different type of cluster, known as a globular, and consists of many more, far older stars. It is relatively close for a globular cluster – just 7200 light years away – and is easily seen through binoculars as a sixth-magnitude blob the size of a Full Moon. Small telescopes will reveal many of the cluster's outlying stars because, for a globular cluster, it is quite loosely packed.

Pavo

Ara was one of the original 48 constellations catalogued by Ptolemy. It is a small and rather inconspicuous constellation said to represent an altar, usually depicted upside down, on which the Greek gods swore their oaths. It is also described as the altar upon which Centaurus was about to sacrifice Lupus the wolf. Sometimes it is shown right-side up with the sacrificial smoke drifting into the Milky Way. The pattern of individual stars is difficult to make out, but the constellation lies to the south of Scorpius, and is crossed by a dense region of the southern Milky Way.

Aries

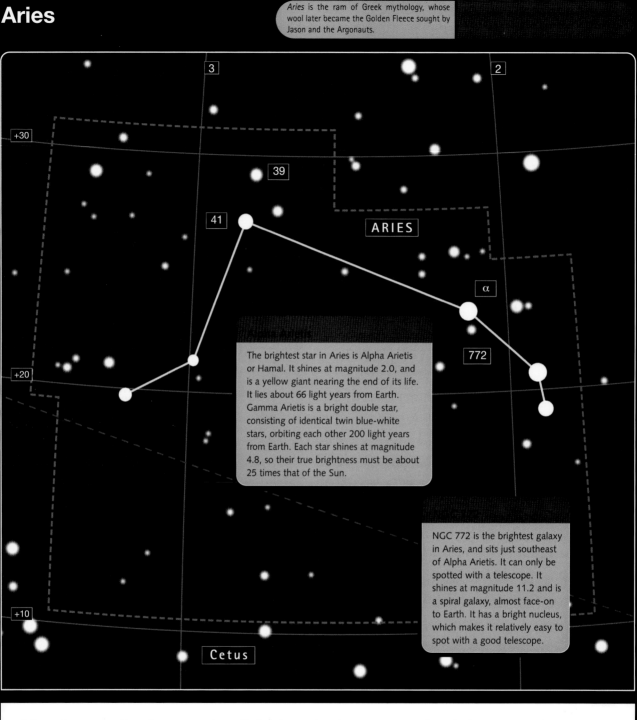

ARIES

3

2

+30

39

41

α

772

+20

Alpha Arietis

The brightest star in Aries is Alpha Arietis or Hamal. It shines at magnitude 2.0, and is a yellow giant nearing the end of its life. It lies about 66 light years from Earth. Gamma Arietis is a bright double star, consisting of identical twin blue-white stars, orbiting each other 200 light years from Earth. Each star shines at magnitude 4.8, so their true brightness must be about 25 times that of the Sun.

NGC 772 is the brightest galaxy in Aries, and sits just southeast of Alpha Arietis. It can only be spotted with a telescope. It shines at magnitude 11.2 and is a spiral galaxy, almost face-on to Earth. It has a bright nucleus, which makes it relatively easy to spot with a good telescope.

+10

Cetus

Aries the ram lies between the distinctive constellations of Andromeda and Taurus. The edge of this constellation used to mark the northern vernal equinox, where the Sun enters the northern half of the sky around 21 March. This point marks the middle of the celestial coordinate system used by astronomers, but the long slow wobble of Earth's axis has today altered the path of the Sun, so that this point, still known as the 'First Point of Aries' now lies in Pisces next door. Aries is a faint group of stars, but lies on the zodiac, so the Sun, Moon, and planets all occasionally pass through it.

Auriga

Auriga is Latin for charioteer, here the legendary Athenian king, Erichthonius, who was said to have invented the chariot.

Only visible at latitudes between 90°N–34°S. Best vision at 10 pm December to February.

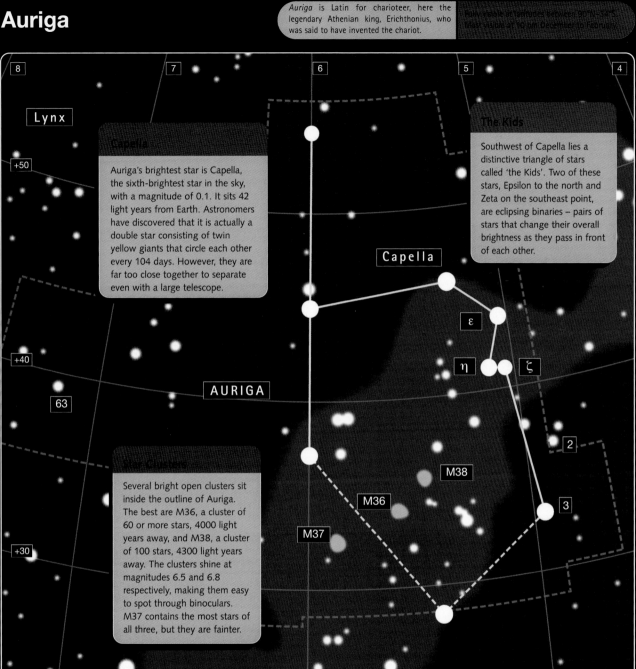

Lynx

Capella

Auriga's brightest star is Capella, the sixth-brightest star in the sky, with a magnitude of 0.1. It sits 42 light years from Earth. Astronomers have discovered that it is actually a double star consisting of twin yellow giants that circle each other every 104 days. However, they are far too close together to separate even with a large telescope.

The Kids

Southwest of Capella lies a distinctive triangle of stars called 'the Kids'. Two of these stars, Epsilon to the north and Zeta on the southeast point, are eclipsing binaries – pairs of stars that change their overall brightness as they pass in front of each other.

Capella

AURIGA

Star Clusters

Several bright open clusters sit inside the outline of Auriga. The best are M36, a cluster of 60 or more stars, 4000 light years away, and M38, a cluster of 100 stars, 4300 light years away. The clusters shine at magnitudes 6.5 and 6.8 respectively, making them easy to spot through binoculars. M37 contains the most stars of all three, but they are fainter.

M38

M36

M37

ε

η

ζ

Auriga is a bright and distinctive constellation. When it is situated high above the horizon, it is a prominent highlight of winter skies in the northern hemisphere. Because the Milky Way passes through it, it is rich in deep-sky objects. Auriga is said to be named after a lame, mythological Athenian king who invented the horse-drawn chariot so he could move about freely. However, mythology does not offer any explanation for the goat and her offspring, or kids, at his left arm. Capella, the name of the brightest star of the constellation, means 'she-goat' in Latin.

Boötes

Boötes represents a man herding the Great and Little Bears (Ursa Major and Ursa Minor) around the night sky with his hunting dogs.

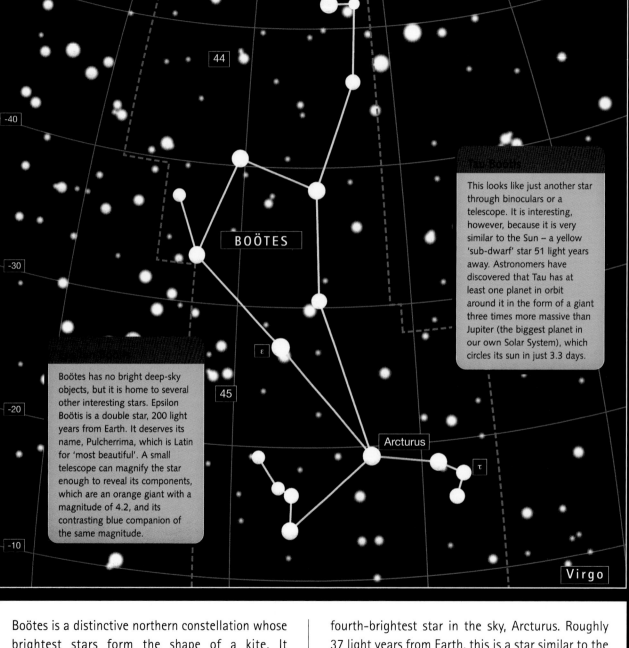

Tau Boötis

This looks like just another star through binoculars or a telescope. It is interesting, however, because it is very similar to the Sun – a yellow 'sub-dwarf' star 51 light years away. Astronomers have discovered that Tau has at least one planet in orbit around it in the form of a giant three times more massive than Jupiter (the biggest planet in our own Solar System), which circles its sun in just 3.3 days.

Boötes has no bright deep-sky objects, but it is home to several other interesting stars. Epsilon Boötis is a double star, 200 light years from Earth. It deserves its name, Pulcherrima, which is Latin for 'most beautiful'. A small telescope can magnify the star enough to reveal its components, which are an orange giant with a magnitude of 4.2, and its contrasting blue companion of the same magnitude.

Arcturus

BOÖTES

Virgo

Boötes is a distinctive northern constellation whose brightest stars form the shape of a kite. It represents a herdsman, driving the bears, Ursa Major and Ursa Minor, across the sky with his hunting dogs (Canes Venatici). The constellation is very easy to spot because its base is marked by the fourth-brightest star in the sky, Arcturus. Roughly 37 light years from Earth, this is a star similar to the Sun, but at the end of its life. It has swollen and brightened to become a red giant, 70 times more luminous and 27 times the diameter of our own star. This will be the Sun's fate in five billion years.

Caelum

Caelum is named after a type of engraving tool used on copper and fine metal.

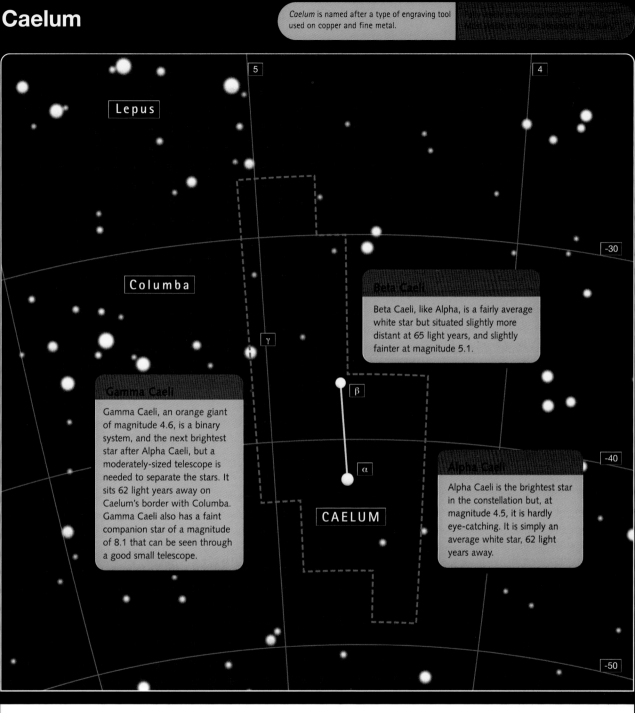

Lepus

5

4

Columba

-30

Beta Caeli

Beta Caeli, like Alpha, is a fairly average white star but situated slightly more distant at 65 light years, and slightly fainter at magnitude 5.1.

γ

Gamma Caeli

Gamma Caeli, an orange giant of magnitude 4.6, is a binary system, and the next brightest star after Alpha Caeli, but a moderately-sized telescope is needed to separate the stars. It sits 62 light years away on Caelum's border with Columba. Gamma Caeli also has a faint companion star of a magnitude of 8.1 that can be seen through a good small telescope.

β

α

CAELUM

-40

Alpha Caeli

Alpha Caeli is the brightest star in the constellation but, at magnitude 4.5, it is hardly eye-catching. It is simply an average white star, 62 light years away.

-50

Caelum is one of the constellations added to the southern sky in the middle of the eighteenth century by Nicolas Louis de Lacaille to fill the southern hemisphere. Many of the constellations added at this time were obscure, and Caelum is one of the least impressive constellations in the entire sky. Its pattern contains just two faint stars, which are said to have been named in honour of the arts to represent an instrument for engraving on copper and fine metals. It lies near the end of the long constellation Eridanus, and west of the brighter stars of Columba, the Dove.

Camelopardalis

Camelopardalis is Latin for a giraffe, but it was originally supposed to represent the camel that carried Rebecca to Isaac in the Old Testament.

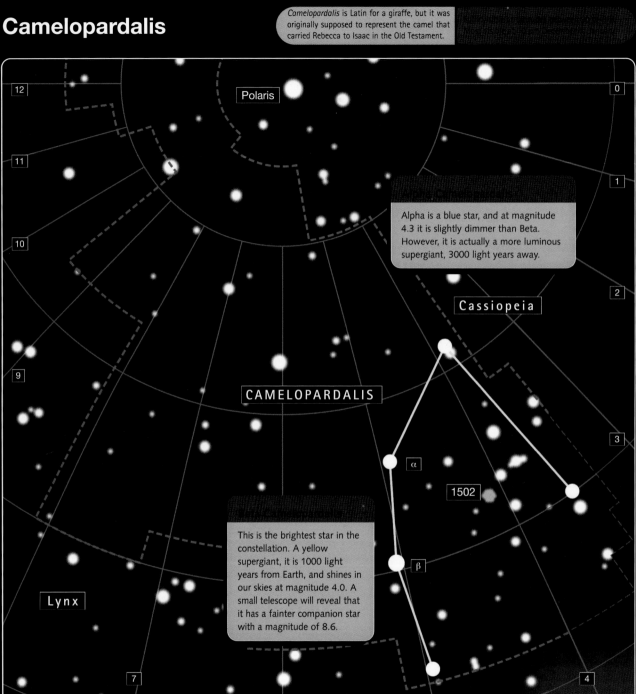

12

Polaris

0

11

1

Alpha is a blue star, and at magnitude 4.3 it is slightly dimmer than Beta. However, it is actually a more luminous supergiant, 3000 light years away.

10

Cassiopeia

2

9

CAMELOPARDALIS

3

α

1502

This is the brightest star in the constellation. A yellow supergiant, it is 1000 light years from Earth, and shines in our skies at magnitude 4.0. A small telescope will reveal that it has a fainter companion star with a magnitude of 8.6.

β

Lynx

7

4

Camelopardalis is a relatively large constellation, but it is not particularly bright. Invented in 1613 by Petrus Plancius, a Dutch astronomer and biblical scholar, Camelopardalis has no mythology associated with it. Plancius claimed that the constellation represented the animal on which

Rebecca rode to marry her husband Isaac in the Old Testament of the Bible, but the name is actually the Latin for giraffe (literally a camel-leopard). Camelopardalis fills a large area of the northern sky between Cassiopeia and Ursa Major, but its brighter stars are concentrated close to Cassiopeia.

Cancer

Cancer represents the mythological crab that came to the aid of the Hydra in battle with Hercules. Hercules crushed the crab underfoot.

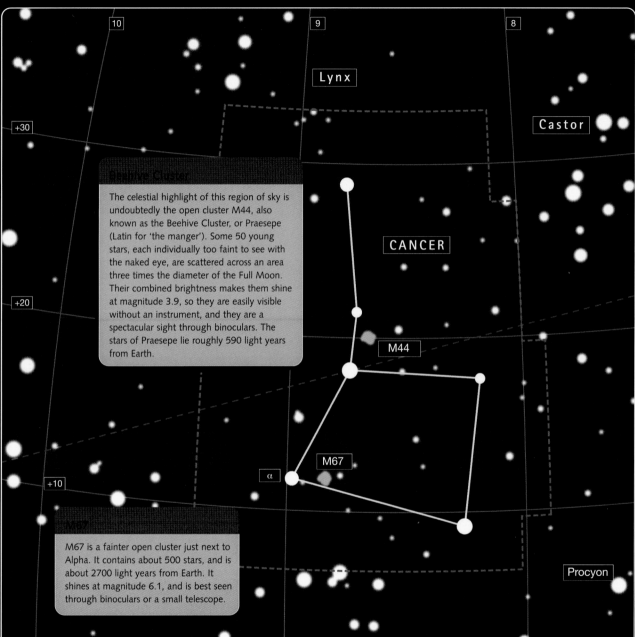

Beehive Cluster

The celestial highlight of this region of sky is undoubtedly the open cluster M44, also known as the Beehive Cluster, or Praesepe (Latin for 'the manger'). Some 50 young stars, each individually too faint to see with the naked eye, are scattered across an area three times the diameter of the Full Moon. Their combined brightness makes them shine at magnitude 3.9, so they are easily visible without an instrument, and they are a spectacular sight through binoculars. The stars of Praesepe lie roughly 590 light years from Earth.

M67

M67 is a fainter open cluster just next to Alpha. It contains about 500 stars, and is about 2700 light years from Earth. It shines at magnitude 6.1, and is best seen through binoculars or a small telescope.

The constellation of Cancer, the Crab, is an extremely ancient constellation. It is a faint grouping of stars lying on the zodiac between the much brighter Gemini and Leo. Galileo was the first to study it with a telescope. It is said to represent a crab, crushed beneath the foot of the hero Hercules.

According to Greek mythology, the second of the twelve labours of Hercules was to kill the nine-headed Hydra. The crab came to the Hydra's aid and bit Hercules' foot. He crushed the crab and, as it had failed to defeat Hercules, the gods only allowed the crab to have faint stars in its constellation.

Canes Venatici

Canes Venatici is Latin for hunting dogs. It is thought to represent the two dogs that Boötes unleashed on the Great and Little Bears.

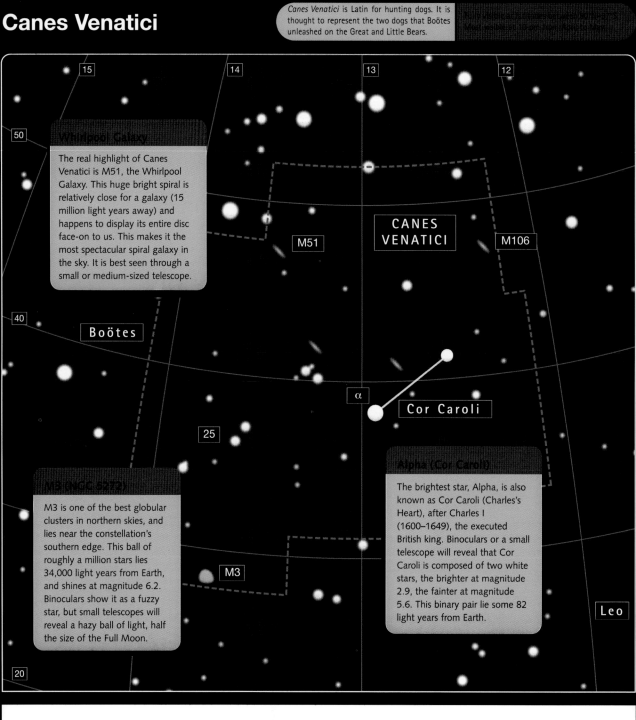

15 **14** **13** **12**

50

Whirlpool Galaxy

The real highlight of Canes Venatici is M51, the Whirlpool Galaxy. This huge bright spiral is relatively close for a galaxy (15 million light years away) and happens to display its entire disc face-on to us. This makes it the most spectacular spiral galaxy in the sky. It is best seen through a small or medium-sized telescope.

CANES VENATICI

M51   M106

40

Boötes

25

α   Cor Caroli

Alpha (Cor Caroli)

The brightest star, Alpha, is also known as Cor Caroli (Charles's Heart), after Charles I (1600–1649), the executed British king. Binoculars or a small telescope will reveal that Cor Caroli is composed of two white stars, the brighter at magnitude 2.9, the fainter at magnitude 5.6. This binary pair lie some 82 light years from Earth.

M3 (NGC 5272)

M3 is one of the best globular clusters in northern skies, and lies near the constellation's southern edge. This ball of roughly a million stars lies 34,000 light years from Earth, and shines at magnitude 6.2. Binoculars show it as a fuzzy star, but small telescopes will reveal a hazy ball of light, half the size of the Full Moon.

M3

Leo

20

This constellation was put together in 1687 by Johannes Hevelius from stars that had once been part of Ursa Major. It is one of three constellations representing dogs, along with Canis Major and Canis Minor. Canes Venatici has no real pattern, but is said to represent Chara and Asterion, the hunting dogs that Boötes, the celestial herdsman, used to chase the Great and Little Bears (Ursa Major and Ursa Minor) around the sky. Although small and indistinct, it contains several interesting objects. It also has a high number of galaxies, which is characteristic of this part of the sky.

Canis Major

Canis Major is Latin for the greater dog and is said to represent the larger of the two dogs following Orion the hunter around the sky.

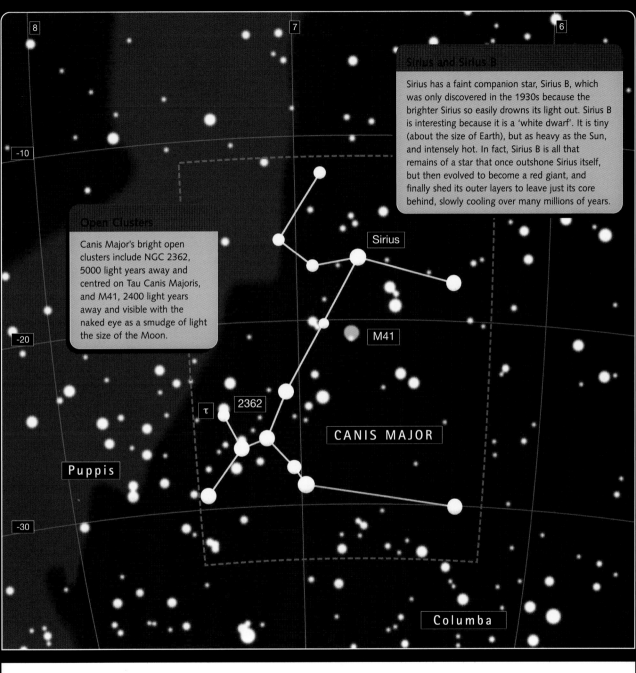

Sirius and Sirius B

Sirius has a faint companion star, Sirius B, which was only discovered in the 1930s because the brighter Sirius so easily drowns its light out. Sirius B is interesting because it is a 'white dwarf'. It is tiny (about the size of Earth), but as heavy as the Sun, and intensely hot. In fact, Sirius B is all that remains of a star that once outshone Sirius itself, but then evolved to become a red giant, and finally shed its outer layers to leave just its core behind, slowly cooling over many millions of years.

Open Clusters

Canis Major's bright open clusters include NGC 2362, 5000 light years away and centred on Tau Canis Majoris, and M41, 2400 light years away and visible with the naked eye as a smudge of light the size of the Moon.

Sirius

M41

2362

τ

CANIS MAJOR

Puppis

Columba

This is one of the most prominent constellations in the night sky. It represents the larger of Orion's two hunting dogs, and is said to be pursuing Lepus the hare or helping Orion fight Taurus the bull. The constellation of Canis Major is home to the brightest star in the sky. It is known as Sirius, meaning 'scorching' because it rose just before the heat of summer. Also called the 'Dog Star', it is an unmistakable sight, shining at magnitude –1.4. Its brightness is largely due to its closeness to Earth – it gives out 23 times the light of the Sun, but is just 8.6 light years away.

Canis Minor

Canis minor is Latin for the lesser dog. The constellation represents the smaller of the two dogs that run with Orion the hunter.

Gemini

Cancer

CANIS MINOR

Procyon

Alpha Canis Minoris (Procyon) shines at magnitude 0.34, making it the eighth-brightest star in the sky. It has a slightly off-white hue, and lies 11.4 light years away from the Earth. So, like Sirius in Canis Major, it is really an average star that appears bright because it happens to lie nearby. The name comes from the Greek for 'before the dog', because from northern latitudes this star rises shortly before Canis Major. Procyon's yellowish tint reveals that its surface is slightly cooler than the pure white Sirius. It also has a lower true luminosity – in reality Procyon is seven times brighter than the Sun, while Sirius is 23 times brighter. This is in keeping with a relationship that all stars follow for most of their lives: the brighter the star, the hotter the surface temperature, and the bluer the appearance.

Hydra

Monoceros

Canis Minor is a small constellation consisting mainly of two stars. Representing the lesser of Orion's two hunting dogs, Canis Minor lies to the south of Gemini from where it follows the hunter Orion. The ancient Greeks did not recognize Canis Minor as a distinct constellation and at first believed that Orion only had one dog. Some thought Canis Minor was a water dog because it stood on the edge of the Milky Way. It is easily located as it contains one of the sky's brightest stars, Procyon. Canis Minor has no deep-sky object brighter than tenth magnitude.

Capricornus

Capricornus means 'that which has horns like a goat' in Latin. It is commonly called the sea goat because it has a tail like a fish.

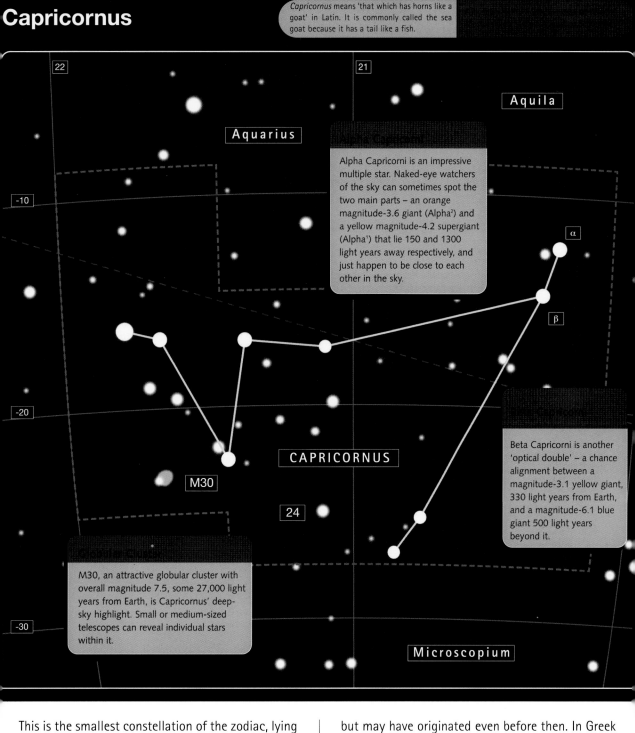

Aquila

Aquarius

Alpha Capricorni

Alpha Capricorni is an impressive multiple star. Naked-eye watchers of the sky can sometimes spot the two main parts – an orange magnitude-3.6 giant (Alpha^2) and a yellow magnitude-4.2 supergiant (Alpha^1) that lie 150 and 1300 light years away respectively, and just happen to be close to each other in the sky.

α

β

CAPRICORNUS

Beta Capricorni is another 'optical double' – a chance alignment between a magnitude-3.1 yellow giant, 330 light years from Earth, and a magnitude-6.1 blue giant 500 light years beyond it.

M30

24

M30, an attractive globular cluster with overall magnitude 7.5, some 27,000 light years from Earth, is Capricornus' deep-sky highlight. Small or medium-sized telescopes can reveal individual stars within it.

Microscopium

This is the smallest constellation of the zodiac, lying between Sagittarius and Aquarius, and is best seen from southern skies. In the northern hemisphere it rises highest in mid- to late summer. There are many myths associated with Capricornus. It was known to the Babylonians and Sumerians of the Middle East but may have originated even before then. In Greek mythology it represents a beast with a goat's head and horns and a fish's tail, known as a 'sea goat'. The Greeks saw it as the goat-horned god Pan, escaping from Typhon the sea monster by turning his lower half into a fish.

Carina

Carina is Latin for keel, specifically the keel of the *Argo*, the ship sailed by Jason and the Argonauts in Greek mythology.

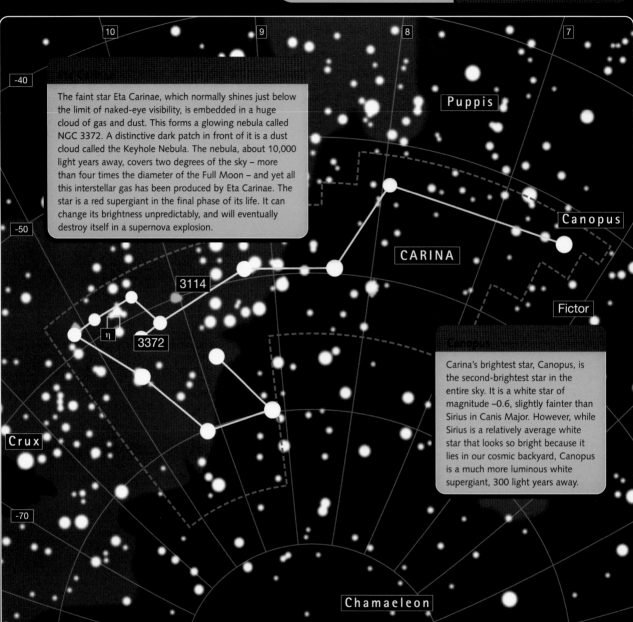

Puppis

Canopus

The faint star Eta Carinae, which normally shines just below the limit of naked-eye visibility, is embedded in a huge cloud of gas and dust. This forms a glowing nebula called NGC 3372. A distinctive dark patch in front of it is a dust cloud called the Keyhole Nebula. The nebula, about 10,000 light years away, covers two degrees of the sky – more than four times the diameter of the Full Moon – and yet all this interstellar gas has been produced by Eta Carinae. The star is a red supergiant in the final phase of its life. It can change its brightness unpredictably, and will eventually destroy itself in a supernova explosion.

CARINA

3114

Fictor

η

3372

Crux

Carina's brightest star, Canopus, is the second-brightest star in the entire sky. It is a white star of magnitude –0.6, slightly fainter than Sirius in Canis Major. However, while Sirius is a relatively average white star that looks so bright because it lies in our cosmic backyard, Canopus is a much more luminous white supergiant, 300 light years away.

Chamaeleon

The constellation of Carina lies in a flourishing part of the Milky Way and is an awe-inspiring constellation. The bright stars in the constellation Carina represent the keel of a ship, the *Argo Navis*, aboard which Jason and his Argonauts sailed in search of the Golden Fleece in Greek mythology.

Along with Vela (the sails) and Puppis (the stern), in Greek times, Carina formed part of a giant single constellation, called Argo Navis. The constellation lies close to the sky's South Pole, and is 'circumpolar'. This means it is never seen to set from much of the Earth's southern hemisphere.

Cassiopeia

Cassiopeia is named after an Ethiopian queen renowned for her vanity. In the constellation she is seated on her throne tidying her hair.

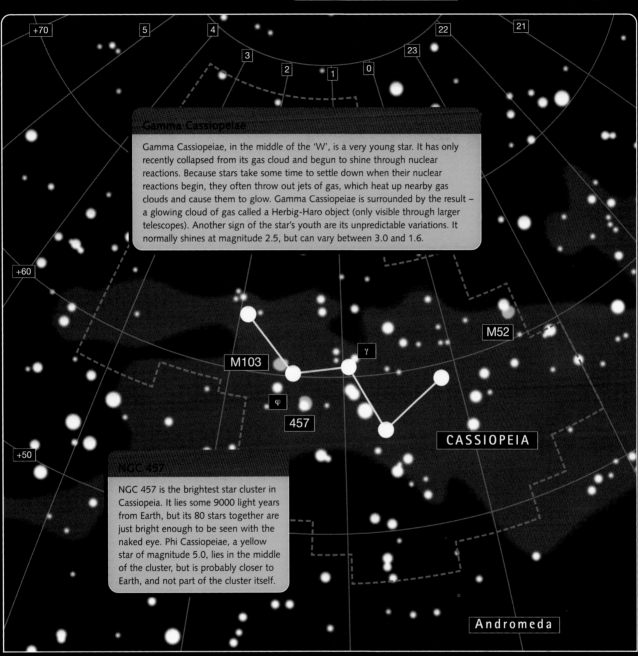

Gamma Cassiopeiae

Gamma Cassiopeiae, in the middle of the 'W', is a very young star. It has only recently collapsed from its gas cloud and begun to shine through nuclear reactions. Because stars take some time to settle down when their nuclear reactions begin, they often throw out jets of gas, which heat up nearby gas clouds and cause them to glow. Gamma Cassiopeiae is surrounded by the result – a glowing cloud of gas called a Herbig-Haro object (only visible through larger telescopes). Another sign of the star's youth are its unpredictable variations. It normally shines at magnitude 2.5, but can vary between 3.0 and 1.6.

M52

M103

457

φ

γ

CASSIOPEIA

Andromeda

NGC 457

NGC 457 is the brightest star cluster in Cassiopeia. It lies some 9000 light years from Earth, but its 80 stars together are just bright enough to be seen with the naked eye. Phi Cassiopeiae, a yellow star of magnitude 5.0, lies in the middle of the cluster, but is probably closer to Earth, and not part of the cluster itself.

Cassiopeia is a familiar sight in northern skies, in the northern reaches of the Milky Way, rich in interesting stars and clusters. It is circumpolar for much of the northern hemisphere, and can be seen throughout the year. Cassiopeia is named for the queen of Ethiopia, and she is depicted sitting on her throne. Famously vain, she boasted that she was fairer than the sea nymphs. As a punishment she was chained to her throne and made to suffer the indignity of hanging upside down for half of the day, which is how the constellation appeared to naked-eye viewers for some of the year.

Centaurs

Centaurus is named for a centaur by the name of Chiron. A mythological being, he had the upper body of a man and the legs of a horse.

14

-30

Alpha Centauri is the third-brightest star in the sky, shining at magnitude –0.3. Good binoculars will show that it is actually a double star, consisting of a yellow star at magnitude 0, and a red one of magnitude 1.3. The pair is orbited by a smaller, fainter and more widely separated red dwarf star, Proxima Centauri, shining at magnitude 11. The Alpha Centauri system contains the three closest stars to Earth. Proxima is the closest of all, at 4.2 light years away, while the Alpha Centauri pair is 0.1 light years farther away.

-40

5128

CENTAURUS

5139

Easily mistaken for a magnitude 3.7 star, but instead of a star-like point, binoculars will reveal it as a fuzzy blob. Omega is actually a huge globular cluster – a ball of several million stars packed into a sphere 650 light years across. Omega Centauri lies 17,000 light years away, and is the largest of the many globular clusters orbiting the Milky Way Galaxy.

-50

Crux

α

-60

13   12

Centaurus is a large, bright southern-hemisphere constellation which was mentioned as far back as the fourth century BC by Eudoxus, the Greek mathematician and astronomer. Its southern reaches lie across the Milky Way, and contain the closest stars to our Solar System, while the northern regions contain the sky's most spectacular globular star cluster. This constellation is one of two in the sky that represent the mythical beasts called Centaurs (the other is Sagittarius). The Centaur in this constellation was believed to be Chiron, a wise Centaur who was tutor to Jason and Hercules.

Cepheus

Cepheus represents the mythological king of Ethiopia, husband of the conceited queen, Cassiopeia, and father of Andromeda.

Polaris

Beta Cephei is yet another variable. It is a prototype of a group of blue stars that show small but rapid changes in brightness. It varies from magnitude 3.2 to 3.3, and is about 600 light years from Earth.

24

β

CEPHEUS

Draco

+60

Delta Cephei

Delta Cephei was the first discovered in a class of stars called Cepheid variables. It is a yellow supergiant with an unstable structure that causes it to swell and shrink between 40 and 46 times the diameter of the Sun in a repeating period of just over five days. This also affects the star's brightness, so it varies between magnitude 3.5 and magnitude 4.4.

δ

μ

The Garnet Star

Mu Cephei is nicknamed the 'Garnet Star' because of its deep red hue. It is a red giant, and the prototype for a type of long-period variable, because it changes its diameter and brightness over a much longer period of 730 days.

+50

Cassiopeia

0

23

22

21

When viewed including fainter, indistinct stars just visible to the naked eye, this constellation seems to be a man wearing a crown. He is King Cepheus, husband of Queen Cassiopeia. However, with respect to the ecliptic, he is upside down and this may relate to the story of Cassiopeia's boast, which led the gods to punish her by making her hang upside down from her throne. The constellation sits close to the sky's North Pole, and so is circumpolar, never setting for much of the northern hemisphere. Cepheus contains several interesting variables (stars that change their brightness over time).

Cetus

The name *Cetus* in Latin means whale, but in this constellation the name refers to a mythological sea monster.

Fully visible at latitudes between 65° N - 79° S
Most visible at 10 pm September to October

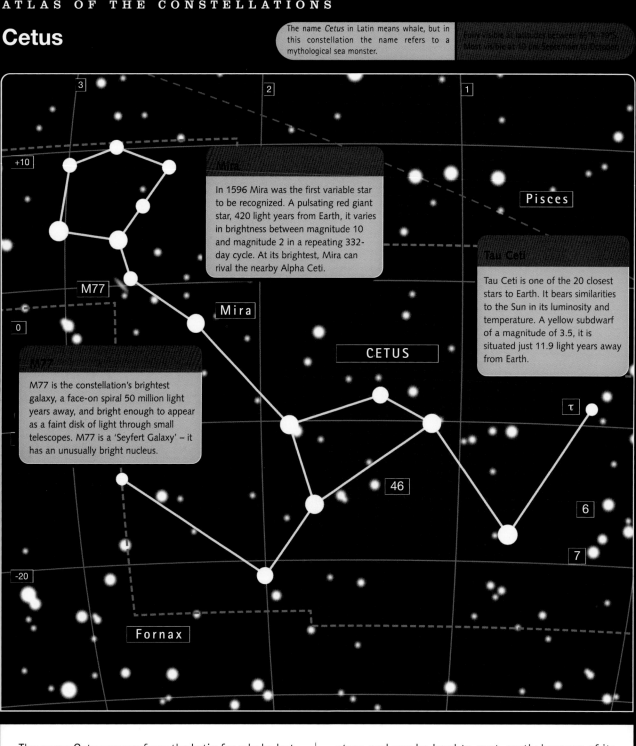

Pisces

Mira

In 1596 Mira was the first variable star to be recognized. A pulsating red giant star, 420 light years from Earth, it varies in brightness between magnitude 10 and magnitude 2 in a repeating 332-day cycle. At its brightest, Mira can rival the nearby Alpha Ceti.

Tau Ceti

Tau Ceti is one of the 20 closest stars to Earth. It bears similarities to the Sun in its luminosity and temperature. A yellow subdwarf of a magnitude of 3.5, it is situated just 11.9 light years away from Earth.

M77

M77 is the constellation's brightest galaxy, a face-on spiral 50 million light years away, and bright enough to appear as a faint disk of light through small telescopes. M77 is a 'Seyfert Galaxy' – it has an unusually bright nucleus.

CETUS

Mira

46

Fornax

+10

0

-20

3   2   1

M77

τ

6

7

The name Cetus comes from the Latin for whale, but the constellation is often depicted as a sea monster. According to the mythology, the goddess Hera sent Cetus to kill Princess Andromeda, but the hero Perseus snatched her from the monster's jaws and saved her. The constellation has no really bright stars, and can be hard to spot, partly because of its most interesting feature, Mira, the variable star. Mira (meaning 'wonderful') is also known as Omicron Ceti. Because it connects the 'head' and 'body' of the sea monster, its brightness can radically change the constellation's appearance.

Chamaeleon

Chamaeleon is the Latin word for chameleon.

Easily visible at latitudes between 7° and 90°.
Best visible at 10 pm from February to May.

Optical Double

Delta is an optical double – an apparent double star that is really two unrelated stars lying on the same line of sight. The closer of the two, Delta[1], is an orange giant star, 360 light years from Earth and shining at magnitude 5.5. The more distant blue Delta[2] outshines Delta[1], at magnitude 4.4, despite being 780 light years away. The two stars are easily separated with binoculars.

True Binary Star

Epsilon, meanwhile, is a true binary star, 290 light years away. A medium-sized telescope can separate its 5.4- and 6.0-magnitude stars.

Volans

ε

δ

-70

CHAMAELEON

3195

NGC 3195

NGC 3195 is a faint ring-like planetary nebula of magnitude 10, best seen using medium-sized telescopes.

Mensa

-80

Lying close to the South Pole, Chamaeleon is a minor southern constellation. It is circumpolar for nearly the entire southern hemisphere. As the name suggests, it represents a chameleon, but the lopsided diamond of faint stars bears no real resemblance to any kind of animal. it was one of twelve constellations first created by Pieter Dirkszoon Keyser and Frederick de Houtman between 1595 and 1597 and was first recorded by Johannes Bayer in his *Uranometria* star atlas of 1603. Being an invention of the 17th century, there is no mythology associated with it.

Circinus

16

15

14

-50

Lupus

Gamma Circini

Gamma Circini is an attractive double system of contrasting stars, but it takes a medium-sized telescope to separate the components. It consists of a blue star with a magnitude of 5.1, and a yellow star with a magnitude of 5.5 orbiting each other about 500 light years away.

Alpha Circini

Alpha Circini, magnitude 3.2, is a white star 65 light years away. Small telescopes easily show its faint, magnitude-8.6 companion. Beta is a white star with a magnitude of 4.1, around 97 light years away.

γ

α

-60

CIRCINUS

Crux

Apus

-70

The obscure constellation of Circinus was crammed into a small gap in the southern skies by the French astronomer, Nicolas Louis de Lacaille, for his star catalogue of 1756. Circinus consists of a narrow triangle of faint stars, which are overpowered by the bright stars of Centaurus, lying directly to their west. It is supposed to represent a pair of compasses as used by surveyors and chartmakers of the time, and is one of a number of constellations that Lacaille named after scientific instruments of different kinds. The constellation is so small that it has few objects of interest.

Columba

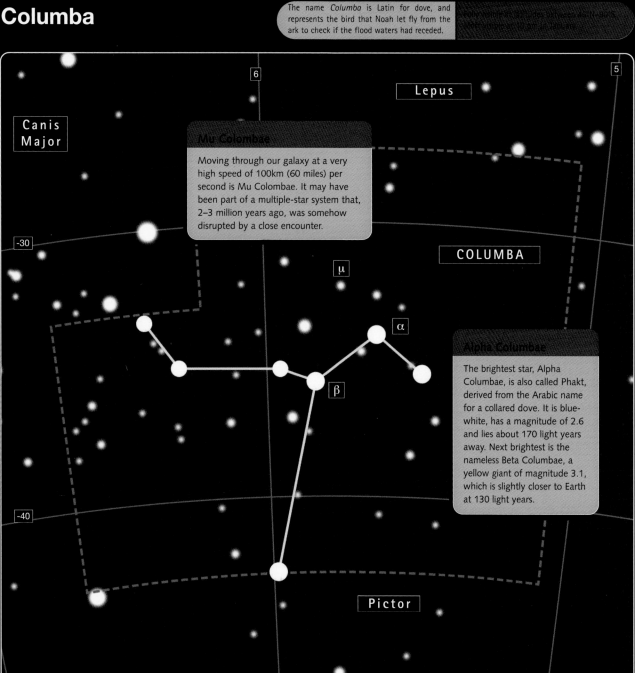

Canis Major

Lepus

6

5

Mu Colombae

Moving through our galaxy at a very high speed of 100km (60 miles) per second is Mu Colombae. It may have been part of a multiple-star system that, 2–3 million years ago, was somehow disrupted by a close encounter.

COLUMBA

-30

μ

α

Alpha Columbae

The brightest star, Alpha Columbae, is also called Phakt, derived from the Arabic name for a collared dove. It is blue-white, has a magnitude of 2.6 and lies about 170 light years away. Next brightest is the nameless Beta Columbae, a yellow giant of magnitude 3.1, which is slightly closer to Earth at 130 light years.

β

-40

Pictor

Dutch astronomer Petrus Plancius created this constellation in 1592, using some 'spare' stars to the southwest of Canis Major. Its name means 'the dove', and since Plancius was a scholar of the Bible, he probably meant it to represent the dove sent out from Noah's ark to find dry land after the flood.

However, others have associated it with a dove sent ahead of Jason's ship, the *Argo*, to find a safe passage into the Black Sea in Greek mythology. Columba is relatively faint and uninteresting, but easy to locate as it lies southwest of the bright stars of Canis Major, and to the north of Carina.

Coma Berenices

The name *Coma Berenices* translates from the Latin as Berenice's hair. Berenice was a queen who reigned in ancient Egypt.

Fully visible at latitudes between 90°N-65°S. Most visible at 10 pm from April to May.

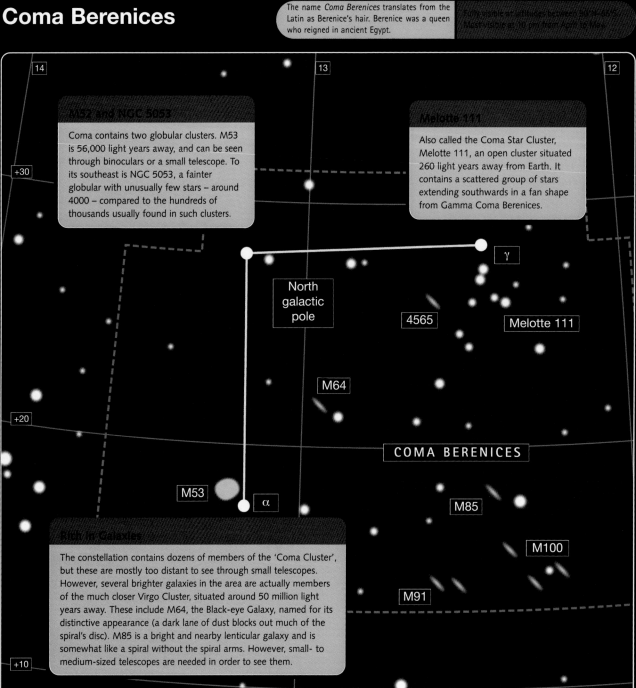

M52 and NGC 5053

Coma contains two globular clusters. M53 is 56,000 light years away, and can be seen through binoculars or a small telescope. To its southeast is NGC 5053, a fainter globular with unusually few stars – around 4000 – compared to the hundreds of thousands usually found in such clusters.

Melotte 111

Also called the Coma Star Cluster, Melotte 111, an open cluster situated 260 light years away from Earth. It contains a scattered group of stars extending southwards in a fan shape from Gamma Coma Berenices.

North galactic pole

γ

4565

Melotte 111

M64

+30

+20

COMA BERENICES

M53

α

M85

M100

Rich in Galaxies

The constellation contains dozens of members of the 'Coma Cluster', but these are mostly too distant to see through small telescopes. However, several brighter galaxies in the area are actually members of the much closer Virgo Cluster, situated around 50 million light years away. These include M64, the Black-eye Galaxy, named for its distinctive appearance (a dark lane of dust blocks out much of the spiral's disc). M85 is a bright and nearby lenticular galaxy and is somewhat like a spiral without the spiral arms. However, small- to medium-sized telescopes are needed in order to see them.

M91

+10

An indistinct constellation situated between Leo and Boötes, Coma Berenices' name means 'Berenice's hair'. It is taken from the name of a queen who reigned over ancient Egypt and promised her hair to Venus, according to mythology, in order to save her husband. The name of the constellation is often shortened to simply 'Coma' and derives from the chain-like appearance of the constellation's many faint stars. Most are part of a cluster called Melotte 111. This is one of the closest open-star clusters to Earth, with about 20 individual stars above the naked eye limit.

Corona Australis

Corona Australis is the Latin term for southern crown. The Greeks saw it as a pretty wreath laying at the forefeet of Sagittarius.

Fully visible at latitudes between 44°N-90°S. Most visible at 10 pm from July to August.

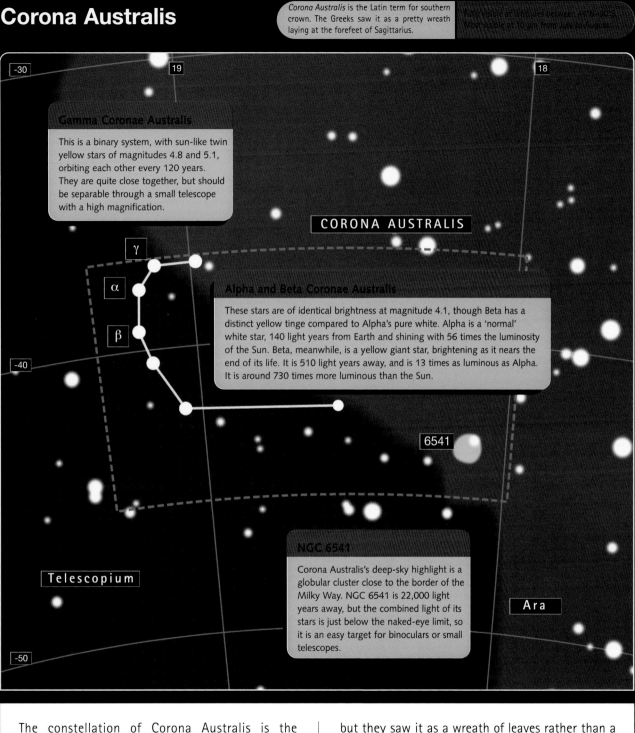

-30 **19** **18**

Gamma Coronae Australis

This is a binary system, with sun-like twin yellow stars of magnitudes 4.8 and 5.1, orbiting each other every 120 years. They are quite close together, but should be separable through a small telescope with a high magnification.

CORONA AUSTRALIS

γ

α

β

Alpha and Beta Coronae Australis

These stars are of identical brightness at magnitude 4.1, though Beta has a distinct yellow tinge compared to Alpha's pure white. Alpha is a 'normal' white star, 140 light years from Earth and shining with 56 times the luminosity of the Sun. Beta, meanwhile, is a yellow giant star, brightening as it nears the end of its life. It is 510 light years away, and is 13 times as luminous as Alpha. It is around 730 times more luminous than the Sun.

-40

6541

NGC 6541

Corona Australis's deep-sky highlight is a globular cluster close to the border of the Milky Way. NGC 6541 is 22,000 light years away, but the combined light of its stars is just below the naked-eye limit, so it is an easy target for binoculars or small telescopes.

Telescopium

Ara

-50

The constellation of Corona Australis is the Southern Crown. It is small but distinctive, and is the southern-hemisphere equivalent of the northern Corona Borealis, although the circlet of stars is not quite as elegant. Even though it is situated so far south it was familiar to the Greeks, but they saw it as a wreath of leaves rather than a crown and believed that it had fallen from the head of the Centaur, Sagittarius, and landed at his feet. The constellation lies on the border of the Milky Way, directly underneath the dense star clouds of Sagittarius.

Corona Borealis

The name *Corona Borealis* is Latin for northern crown, sometimes thought to represent the crown that Dionysus gave to Ariadne.

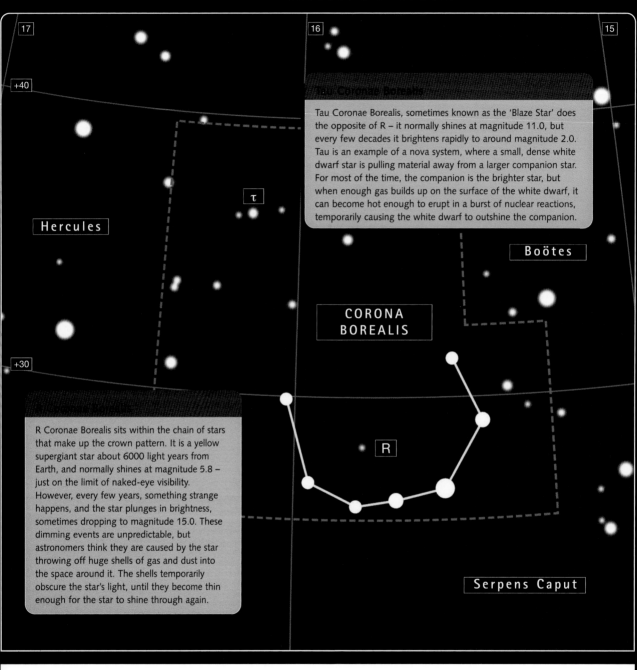

Tau Coronae Borealis

Tau Coronae Borealis, sometimes known as the 'Blaze Star' does the opposite of R – it normally shines at magnitude 11.0, but every few decades it brightens rapidly to around magnitude 2.0. Tau is an example of a nova system, where a small, dense white dwarf star is pulling material away from a larger companion star. For most of the time, the companion is the brighter star, but when enough gas builds up on the surface of the white dwarf, it can become hot enough to erupt in a burst of nuclear reactions, temporarily causing the white dwarf to outshine the companion.

Hercules

Boötes

CORONA BOREALIS

R Coronae Borealis

R Coronae Borealis sits within the chain of stars that make up the crown pattern. It is a yellow supergiant star about 6000 light years from Earth, and normally shines at magnitude 5.8 – just on the limit of naked-eye visibility. However, every few years, something strange happens, and the star plunges in brightness, sometimes dropping to magnitude 15.0. These dimming events are unpredictable, but astronomers think they are caused by the star throwing off huge shells of gas and dust into the space around it. The shells temporarily obscure the star's light, until they become thin enough for the star to shine through again.

Serpens Caput

The constellation Corona Borealis was at first simply called Corona, but Borealis (Northern) was added on later to contrast with the Southern Crown (Corona Australis). Corona Borealis was sometimes thought to be the crown that was given to Ariadne, daughter of Minos of Crete, by the god Dionysus in mythology. At other times it was thought to belong to Boötes, the herdsman. The constellation lies east of Boötes in the northern skies. Its stars are relatively faint, but its shape makes it distinctive and easy to spot. Its most interesting objects are two variable stars. It has no bright deep-sky objects.

Corvus

The name *Corvus* is Latin for raven or crow. This constellation is named after the crow perched on the coils of Hydra, the multi-headed snake.

13

12

NGC 4038 and 4039

Right against the border with Crater lie the spiral galaxies NGC 4038 and 4039. Although they are barely visible through small telescopes, these galaxies are fascinating because they are colliding with each other. The shock waves where their gas clouds are forced against each other have triggered a tremendous burst of star formation between the galaxies, while gravitational forces have flung their spiral arms out into intergalactic space, where they form two long streamers. This gives the galaxies their common name of 'The Antennae'.

-10

Virgo

Crater

β

γ

CORVUS

4038

4039

-20

Delta Corvi

Delta is a double star, with a blue-white component of magnitude 3.1, accompanied by a magnitude-8.5 companion of an unusual shade: many observers have described it as purple. The entire system is about 100 light years away.

δ

α

Hydra

-30

The constellation of Corvus, the crow, forms a distinct skewed square to the southwest of the bright star Spica in Virgo. It sits on the long snaking back of Hydra, the water snake, and is linked to it in the Greek legends (see Crater).

As in several other constellations, Johannes Bayer got his initial naming wrong when he applied Greek letters to the stars of Corvus. The constellation's brightest star is actually Gamma, a blue-white star, 220 light years from Earth, which shines at magnitude 2.6. Beta, a yellow giant, is just slightly fainter and is 265 light years away.

Crater

Crater is the Latin name for cup or chalice. This constellation represents the cup that the Crow (*Corvus*) used to collect water for Apollo.

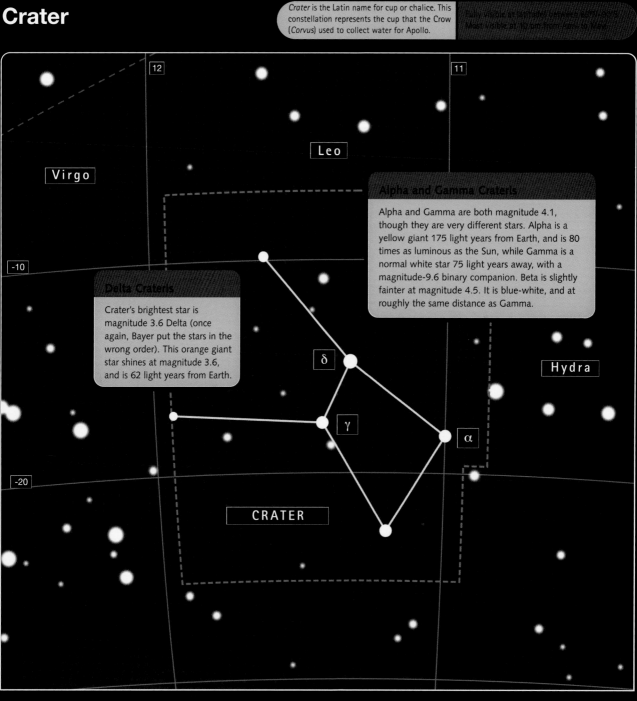

Leo

Virgo

Alpha and Gamma Crateris

Alpha and Gamma are both magnitude 4.1, though they are very different stars. Alpha is a yellow giant 175 light years from Earth, and is 80 times as luminous as the Sun, while Gamma is a normal white star 75 light years away, with a magnitude-9.6 binary companion. Beta is slightly fainter at magnitude 4.5. It is blue-white, and at roughly the same distance as Gamma.

Delta Crateris

Crater's brightest star is magnitude 3.6 Delta (once again, Bayer put the stars in the wrong order). This orange giant star shines at magnitude 3.6, and is 62 light years from Earth.

Hydra

δ

γ

α

CRATER

Crater is a very faint yet distinctive constellation representing a chalice or cup belonging to the Greek god Apollo. It lies just to the west of Corvus, the crow, and on the 'back' of Hydra, the water snake. All three constellations are linked by the same legend: Apollo sent the crow to fetch water in the cup, but it was distracted along the way. The crow blamed the water snake for the delay, saying that it had blocked the well. Apollo saw through the lie, and flung cup, crow and snake into the sky. The bow-tie of the brightest stars, and position just to the south of Leo, makes Crater fairly easy to identify.

Crux

The Jewel Box

The constellation's most spectacular features are a star cluster and a nebula that lie next to each other. NGC 4755 is a beautiful open cluster centred on the blue supergiant star Kappa Crucis. To the naked eye it appears as a fuzzy star of magnitude 4.0, but binoculars will show a scattering of several dozen, mostly blue-white, stars, with a startling contrast created by a red supergiant near the middle. Nineteenth-century British astronomer John Herschel named the cluster 'The Jewel Box' because of its beauty. It is 7600 light years away.

CRUX

Vela

Lupus

4755

α

Alpha Crucis

Alpha Crucis or Acrux, at the southern end of the cross, is a blue-white double star, 320 light years from Earth, with an overall magnitude of 0.8. Beta, or Becrux, is a single, slightly variable blue-white star, around magnitude 1.2 and 350 light years away.

Apus

Crux, the Southern Cross, is the smallest constellation in the sky. However, it is one of the most famous and easy to recognize because of the distinct pattern formed by its four bright stars. It lies in the heart of the southern Milky Way in a region of real brilliance, and is circumpolar for much of the southern hemisphere. The stars were known to the ancient Greeks, who saw Crux as part of Centaurus. In the 16th century it was recognized as a constellation in its own right after Amerigo Vespucci mapped the stars of Crux during his expedition to South America in 1501.

Cygnus

The name *Cygnus* is Latin for swan. Here, it is the swan that Zeus transformed himself into in order to procreate with Queen Leda of Sparta.

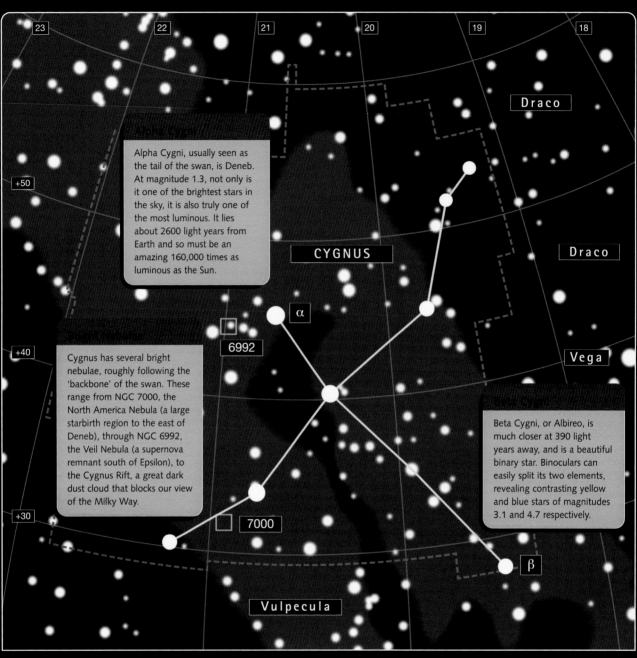

Alpha Cygni

Alpha Cygni, usually seen as the tail of the swan, is Deneb. At magnitude 1.3, not only is it one of the brightest stars in the sky, it is also truly one of the most luminous. It lies about 2600 light years from Earth and so must be an amazing 160,000 times as luminous as the Sun.

Cygnus has several bright nebulae, roughly following the 'backbone' of the swan. These range from NGC 7000, the North America Nebula (a large starbirth region to the east of Deneb), through NGC 6992, the Veil Nebula (a supernova remnant south of Epsilon), to the Cygnus Rift, a great dark dust cloud that blocks our view of the Milky Way.

Beta Cygni, or Albireo, is much closer at 390 light years away, and is a beautiful binary star. Binoculars can easily split its two elements, revealing contrasting yellow and blue stars of magnitudes 3.1 and 4.7 respectively.

Draco

Draco

CYGNUS

Vega

α

6992

7000

β

Vulpecula

One of the northern sky's most impressive constellations, Cygnus, the Swan, is also sometimes called the Northern Cross. It lies across a rich, bright region of the Milky Way, and is easy to locate, passing high overhead for most of the northern hemisphere on summer nights. Civilizations as far back as the Chaldeans have seen this constellation as a bird. According to the Greek mythology, this constellation represents the swan that the god Zeus transformed himself into in order to seduce Queen Leda of Sparta. Their union subsequently created the twins Castor and Pollux, as well as Helen of Troy.

Delphinus

The name *Delphinus* is Latin for dolphin. The dolphin of this constellation is associated with at least two separate legends.

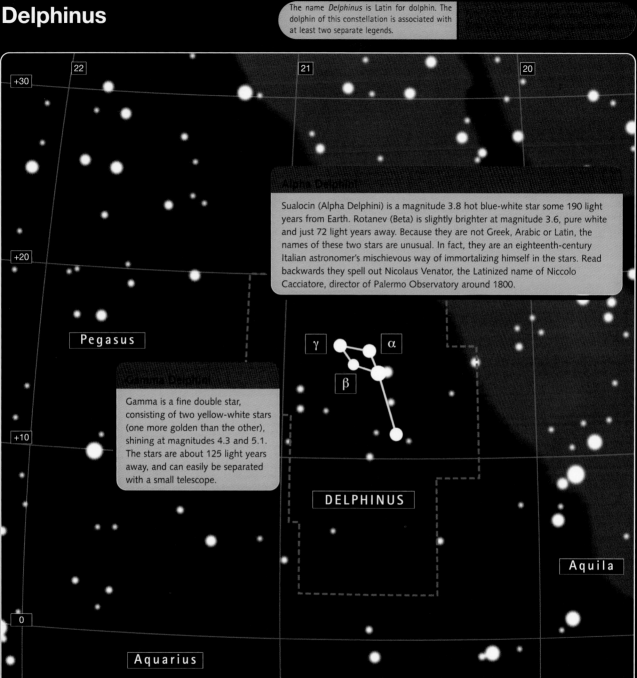

Alpha Delphini

Sualocin (Alpha Delphini) is a magnitude 3.8 hot blue-white star some 190 light years from Earth. Rotanev (Beta) is slightly brighter at magnitude 3.6, pure white and just 72 light years away. Because they are not Greek, Arabic or Latin, the names of these two stars are unusual. In fact, they are an eighteenth-century Italian astronomer's mischievous way of immortalizing himself in the stars. Read backwards they spell out Nicolaus Venator, the Latinized name of Niccolo Cacciatore, director of Palermo Observatory around 1800.

Gamma Delphini

Gamma is a fine double star, consisting of two yellow-white stars (one more golden than the other), shining at magnitudes 4.3 and 5.1. The stars are about 125 light years away, and can easily be separated with a small telescope.

This small but distinctive constellation lies just north of the celestial equator, in a rich area of the Milky Way between Pegasus and Aquila. It represents a dolphin from Greek mythology. According to one legend, Delphinus was a messenger of the sea god Poseidon that saved the life of the poet and musician Arion, the player of the lyre represented by nearby Lyra. Another legend suggests that Poseidon sent Delphinus to fetch the mermaid Amphitrite and convince her to marry Poseidon. Delphinus is easily spotted as four of its five bright stars make up a compact diamond shape.

Dorado

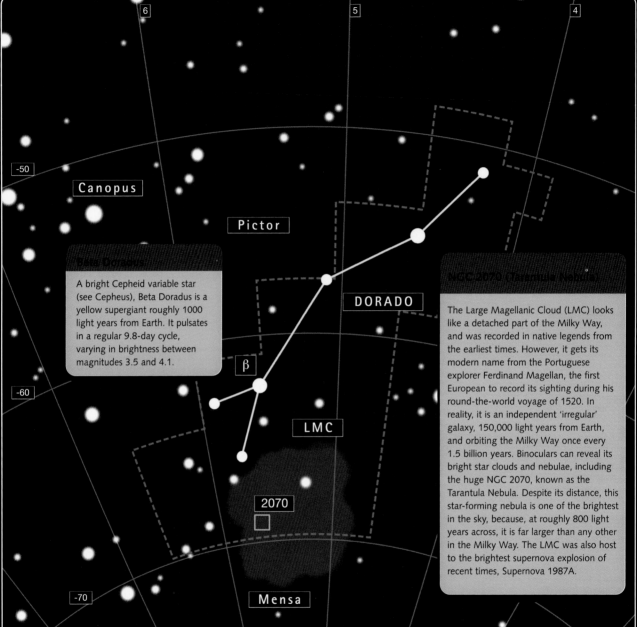

Beta Doradus

A bright Cepheid variable star (see Cepheus), Beta Doradus is a yellow supergiant roughly 1000 light years from Earth. It pulsates in a regular 9.8-day cycle, varying in brightness between magnitudes 3.5 and 4.1.

NGC 2070 (Tarantula Nebula)

The Large Magellanic Cloud (LMC) looks like a detached part of the Milky Way, and was recorded in native legends from the earliest times. However, it gets its modern name from the Portuguese explorer Ferdinand Magellan, the first European to record its sighting during his round-the-world voyage of 1520. In reality, it is an independent 'irregular' galaxy, 150,000 light years from Earth, and orbiting the Milky Way once every 1.5 billion years. Binoculars can reveal its bright star clouds and nebulae, including the huge NGC 2070, known as the Tarantula Nebula. Despite its distance, this star-forming nebula is one of the brightest in the sky, because, at roughly 800 light years across, it is far larger than any other in the Milky Way. The LMC was also host to the brightest supernova explosion of recent times, Supernova 1987A.

Dorado is one of a group of southern constellations representing exotic animals. It was among 12 constellations created by Pieter Dirkszoon Keyser and Frederick de Houtman between 1595 and 1597, and it first appeared in Johannes Bayer's *Uranometria* in 1603. Dorado is a constellation with a relatively faint pattern of stars to the west of Carina, and is circumpolar for much of the southern hemisphere. Although its stars are not spectacular, Dorado is host to our brightest satellite galaxy, the Large Magellanic Cloud (LMC), one of the most interesting objects in the night sky.

Draco

The name *Draco* is Latin for dragon. It is named after the dragon that guarded the golden apples of the daughters of Atlas.

Fully visible at latitudes between 90°N–4°S. Most visible at 10 pm March to September.

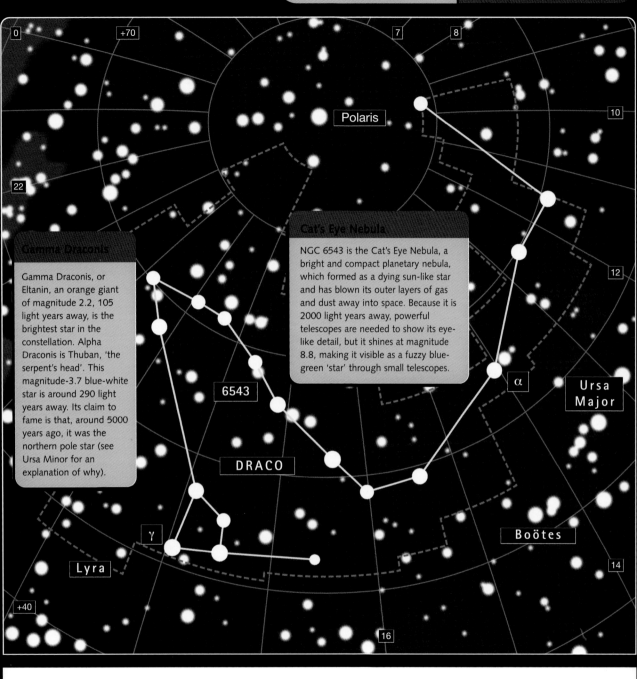

Polaris

Cat's Eye Nebula

NGC 6543 is the Cat's Eye Nebula, a bright and compact planetary nebula, which formed as a dying sun-like star and has blown its outer layers of gas and dust away into space. Because it is 2000 light years away, powerful telescopes are needed to show its eye-like detail, but it shines at magnitude 8.8, making it visible as a fuzzy blue-green 'star' through small telescopes.

Gamma Draconis

Gamma Draconis, or Eltanin, an orange giant of magnitude 2.2, 105 light years away, is the brightest star in the constellation. Alpha Draconis is Thuban, 'the serpent's head'. This magnitude-3.7 blue-white star is around 290 light years away. Its claim to fame is that, around 5000 years ago, it was the northern pole star (see Ursa Minor for an explanation of why).

6543

DRACO

α

Ursa Major

γ

Boötes

Lyra

Draco, the constellation of the Dragon, lies in the far north of the sky and consists of a long chain of relatively faint stars, curling themselves much of the way around the North Celestial Pole. In mythology, it is said to represent the dragon that guarded the golden apples of the Hesperides, who were the daughters of Atlas. The dragon was ultimately slain by Hercules as one of the Twelve Labours he was forced to perform. For most of the northern hemisphere, Draco never sets. It lies far from the Milky Way, yet contains several interesting objects. However, it has no truly prominent stars.

Equuleus

The name *Equuleus* is Latin for little horse or foal, in this instance, possibly the foal Celaris, brother of the winged horse Pegasus.

22   21

+20

Gamma Equulei

Gamma is an average white star, about 120 light years away and magnitude 4.7. Binoculars will show that there is another star next door to it in the sky at just below naked-eye visibility, but the two stars are a mere chance alignment, and not physically related.

Pegasus

+10

γ

Epsilon Equulei

Epsilon Equulei is a triple star, arising from a line-of-sight effect and a genuine binary system. Small telescopes will reveal the 'optical double' – a star with a creamy hue and magnitude of 5.4, 200 light years away, alongside a magnitude-7.4 star of a similar shade that, despite its fainter appearance, is considerably closer to us at 125 light years away. The brighter star is itself a binary composed of two almost identical stars, but these are so close together that they merge into one through most amateur telescopes.

α

ε

EQUULEUS

Alpha Equulei

Kitalpha (Alpha Equulei) is the brightest star, at magnitude 3.9. It is 190 light years from Earth, and is a yellow giant that is 75 times more luminous than the Sun. Beta is a white star of magnitude 5.2, 360 light years away.

0

Aquarius

Equuleus, the little horse, is the second-smallest constellation in the sky. It is the only constellation that is smaller than Crux. It is an inconspicuous rectangle of faint stars to the west of Pegasus, a much larger horse. Despite its insignificant size and lack of bright stars, this constellation dates back to ancient Greek times and was one of Ptolemy's 48 constellations According to Greek mythology it represents the foal Celaris, which Mercury gave to Castor. It is relatively easy to locate, because it is situated between the bright star Epsilon Pegasi and the distinctive pattern of Delphinus.

Eridanus

Eridanus comes from the River Eridanus, which appears in the story of Phaëton, who fell into the river after trying to drive Helios' chariot.

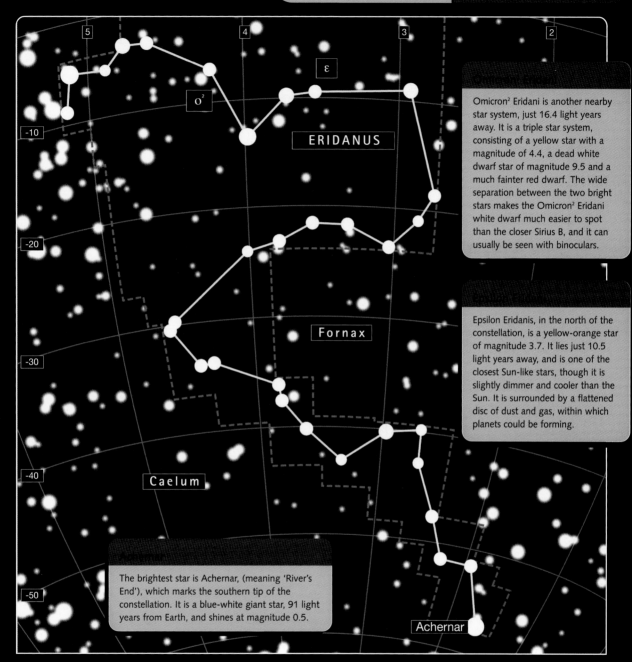

ERIDANUS

Fornax

Caelum

Omicron² Eridani

Omicron² Eridani is another nearby star system, just 16.4 light years away. It is a triple star system, consisting of a yellow star with a magnitude of 4.4, a dead white dwarf star of magnitude 9.5 and a much fainter red dwarf. The wide separation between the two bright stars makes the Omicron² Eridani white dwarf much easier to spot than the closer Sirius B, and it can usually be seen with binoculars.

Epsilon Eridani

Epsilon Eridanis, in the north of the constellation, is a yellow-orange star of magnitude 3.7. It lies just 10.5 light years away, and is one of the closest Sun-like stars, though it is slightly dimmer and cooler than the Sun. It is surrounded by a flattened disc of dust and gas, within which planets could be forming.

Achernar

The brightest star is Achernar, (meaning 'River's End'), which marks the southern tip of the constellation. It is a blue-white giant star, 91 light years from Earth, and shines at magnitude 0.5.

Achernar

Eridanus, the celestial river, is a huge but indistinct constellation that stretches from its northern source near Orion down towards the South Celestial Pole. Most of its stars are quite faint, but some are still interesting, and there are a number of deep-sky objects along its length. Because of the path it follows it is associated with two myths. One is that it is the River Eridanus flowing into Aquarius. It is also connected with Phaëton, who grabbed the reins of the sun god Helios' chariot and veered uncontrollably in different directions, getting too close to Earth and burning people's skin.

Fornax

The name *Fornax* is Latin for furnace. It was first introduced by Nicolas Louis de Lacaille as *Fornax Chemica*, meaning chemists' furnace.

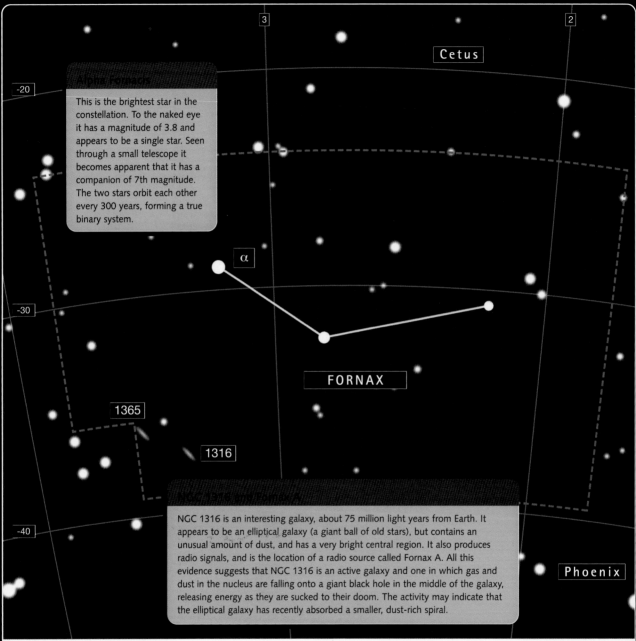

Cetus

Alpha Fornacis

This is the brightest star in the constellation. To the naked eye it has a magnitude of 3.8 and appears to be a single star. Seen through a small telescope it becomes apparent that it has a companion of 7th magnitude. The two stars orbit each other every 300 years, forming a true binary system.

α

FORNAX

1365

1316

NGC 1316 and Fornax A

NGC 1316 is an interesting galaxy, about 75 million light years from Earth. It appears to be an elliptical galaxy (a giant ball of old stars), but contains an unusual amount of dust, and has a very bright central region. It also produces radio signals, and is the location of a radio source called Fornax A. All this evidence suggests that NGC 1316 is an active galaxy and one in which gas and dust in the nucleus are falling onto a giant black hole in the middle of the galaxy, releasing energy as they are sucked to their doom. The activity may indicate that the elliptical galaxy has recently absorbed a smaller, dust-rich spiral.

Phoenix

This constellation is not highly distinguished and lies in an unremarkable area of sky. It was invented by the French astronomer Nicolas Louis de Lacaille in the middle of the eighteenth century. Originally he introduced it as Fornax Chemica, or the Chemists' Furnace. The winding path of Eridanus largely surrounds it, and it sits on the southern border of Cetus. None of its stars are brighter than fourth magnitude. Fornax has recently been described as being on Earth's doorstep because Alpha Fornacis, a double star in the constellation, is only about 46 light years away from us.

Gemini

The name *Gemini* is Latin for twins. Here the twins are two bright stars named after Castor and Pollux, who lean towards each other.

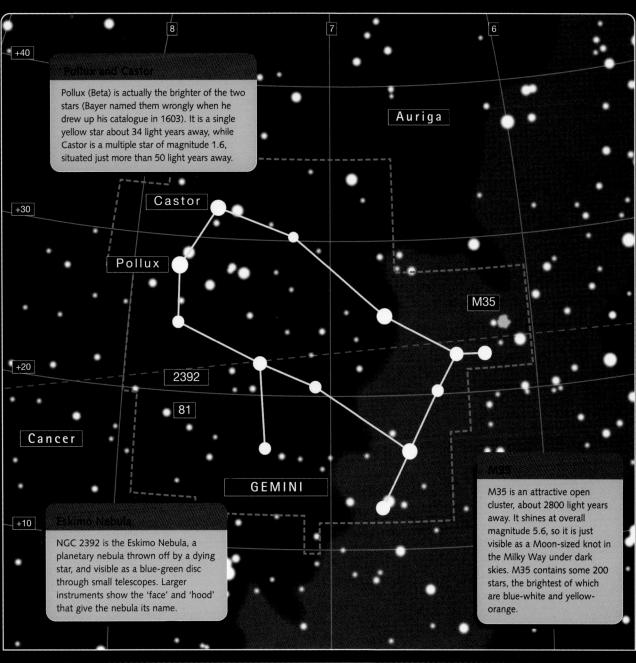

Pollux and Castor

Pollux (Beta) is actually the brighter of the two stars (Bayer named them wrongly when he drew up his catalogue in 1603). It is a single yellow star about 34 light years away, while Castor is a multiple star of magnitude 1.6, situated just more than 50 light years away.

Eskimo Nebula

NGC 2392 is the Eskimo Nebula, a planetary nebula thrown off by a dying star, and visible as a blue-green disc through small telescopes. Larger instruments show the 'face' and 'hood' that give the nebula its name.

M35

M35 is an attractive open cluster, about 2800 light years away. It shines at overall magnitude 5.6, so it is just visible as a Moon-sized knot in the Milky Way under dark skies. M35 contains some 200 stars, the brightest of which are blue-white and yellow-orange.

Gemini, the Twins, is a bright constellation of northern winter skies, lying between Taurus and Cancer. It lies on the Zodiac, so planets are sometimes found here. The Milky Way also passes through it, so it contains several interesting deep-sky objects. Even to the naked eye, Gemini is easy to envision as two parallel stick figures. The brightest stars, Alpha and Beta, are called Castor and Pollux. Greek mythology surrounding these twins involves the theft of cattle because the Milky Way nearby was once thought to be a herd of cows. The entire system lies about 52 light years from Earth.

Grus

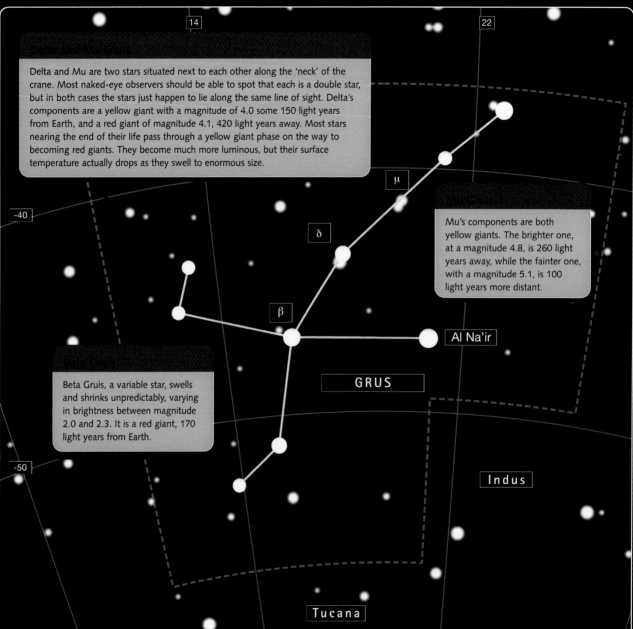

Delta and Mu Gruis

Delta and Mu are two stars situated next to each other along the 'neck' of the crane. Most naked-eye observers should be able to spot that each is a double star, but in both cases the stars just happen to lie along the same line of sight. Delta's components are a yellow giant with a magnitude of 4.0 some 150 light years from Earth, and a red giant of magnitude 4.1, 420 light years away. Most stars nearing the end of their life pass through a yellow giant phase on the way to becoming red giants. They become much more luminous, but their surface temperature actually drops as they swell to enormous size.

Mu's components are both yellow giants. The brighter one, at a magnitude 4.8, is 260 light years away, while the fainter one, with a magnitude 5.1, is 100 light years more distant.

Beta Gruis, a variable star, swells and shrinks unpredictably, varying in brightness between magnitude 2.0 and 2.3. It is a red giant, 170 light years from Earth.

GRUS

Al Na'ir

Indus

Tucana

The southern constellation of Grus is one of the 12 constellations named by Dutch navigators Frederick de Houtman and Pieter Dirkszoon Keyser during their explorations of the 1590s. It represents a long-necked flying crane, and the bright stars Alpha and Beta make it relatively easy to locate. The Arabic names of some of its stars reflect the fact that, until the 17th century, Grus was thought to be a part of Piscis Austrinus and there is no earlier mythology associated with it. It contains no deep-sky objects, but has a number of interesting double stars; none of the bright ones are true binaries.

Hercules

Hercules is named after the Roman name for the Greek mythological hero, Herakles, who was the demigod son of Zeus and Alcmene.

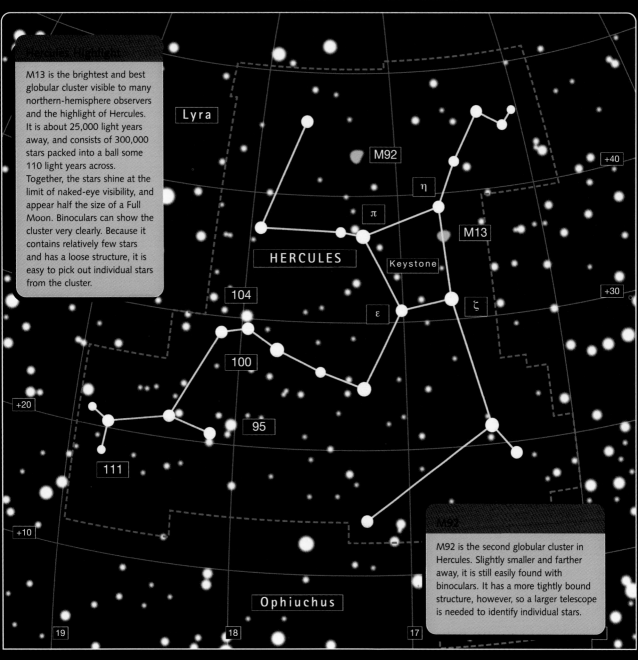

Hercules Highlight

M13 is the brightest and best globular cluster visible to many northern-hemisphere observers and the highlight of Hercules. It is about 25,000 light years away, and consists of 300,000 stars packed into a ball some 110 light years across. Together, the stars shine at the limit of naked-eye visibility, and appear half the size of a Full Moon. Binoculars can show the cluster very clearly. Because it contains relatively few stars and has a loose structure, it is easy to pick out individual stars from the cluster.

M92

M92 is the second globular cluster in Hercules. Slightly smaller and farther away, it is still easily found with binoculars. It has a more tightly bound structure, however, so a larger telescope is needed to identify individual stars.

Hercules is the fifth-largest constellation in the sky, depicting the hero of Greek mythology, who was ordered to perform 12 labours. Here he is depicted kneeling on the head of the dragon Draco (the figure is 'upside down' in the skies of the northern hemisphere), which he had to slay as one of his labours. Other constellations are associated with the labours as well as Draco – Cancer and Hydra, for example. Despite its size, the constellation's pattern can be difficult to spot. It is best to start with the four stars of the Keystone and then find each of the figure's limbs.

Horologium

Horologium is the Latin name for clock and was first named in honour of Christiaan Huygens, inventor of the pendulum clock.

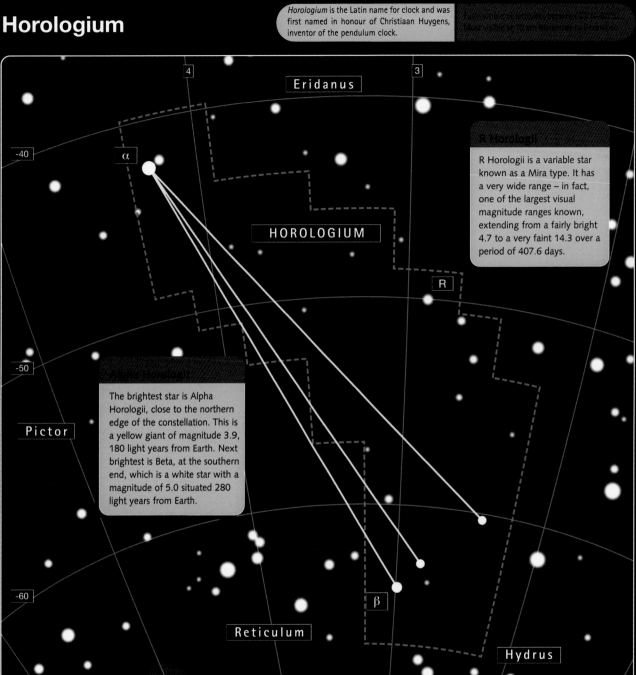

R Horologii

R Horologii is a variable star known as a Mira type. It has a very wide range – in fact, one of the largest visual magnitude ranges known, extending from a fairly bright 4.7 to a very faint 14.3 over a period of 407.6 days.

The brightest star is Alpha Horologii, close to the northern edge of the constellation. This is a yellow giant of magnitude 3.9, 180 light years from Earth. Next brightest is Beta, at the southern end, which is a white star with a magnitude of 5.0 situated 280 light years from Earth.

Horologium is an obscure constellation that fills the sky directly east of the southern end of Eridanus. It represents a clock, but, like many of Nicolas Louis de Lacaille's other constellations, it has no real structure. It was originally called Horologium Oscillitorium in honour of Christiaan Huygens, the inventor of the pendulum clock, and some artists have drawn the constellation as a swinging pendulum, suspended at the north end. However, the name has since been shortened to the simpler Horologium. It was not visible in the Mediterranean so there is no early mythology associated with it.

Hydra

Hydra is the name for the multi-headed water snake of Greek mythology that Hercules had to slay as one of his Twelve Labours.

Fully within latitudes between 64°N–83°S. Best visible at 10 pm from February to June.

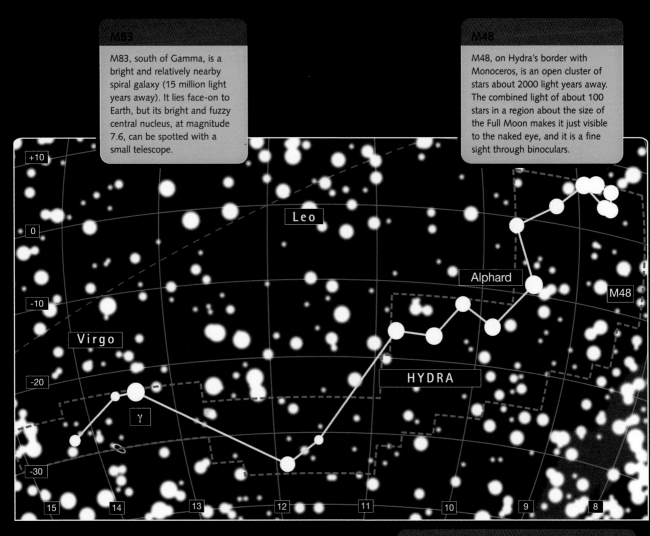

M83

M83, south of Gamma, is a bright and relatively nearby spiral galaxy (15 million light years away). It lies face-on to Earth, but its bright and fuzzy central nucleus, at magnitude 7.6, can be spotted with a small telescope.

M48

M48, on Hydra's border with Monoceros, is an open cluster of stars about 2000 light years away. The combined light of about 100 stars in a region about the size of the Full Moon makes it just visible to the naked eye, and it is a fine sight through binoculars.

Leo

Virgo

Alphard

HYDRA

M48

γ

Gamma Hydrae

Gamma Hydrae, towards the snake's tail end, is the second-brightest star. It is a yellow giant of magnitude 3.0, and is about 100 light years from Earth.

Alphard (Alpha Hydrae)

Alphard's name means 'the solitary one', and is the brightest star in quite a large region of sky. A giant star some 65 light years away, it shines with an orange light at magnitude 2.0.

The constellation of Hydra, the water snake, is the largest in the sky, but it could hardly be called prominent. Its faint stars make it difficult to trace the snake's winding path across the sky south of constellations such as Virgo, Corvus and Crater. The most distinctive region is the snake's head, a wedge-shaped group of six stars south of Cancer. To their southeast lies Alphard, the constellation's brightest star, marking the snake's heart. In Greek mythology Hydra is not only associated with Hercules but is accused by Corvus the crow of blocking a well, incurring Apollo's wrath.

Hydrus

Hydrus is the Latin name for a male water snake or 'little Hydra'. It should not be confused with Hydra, an entirely different constellation.

VW Hydri, which lies northeast of Gamma, is a cataclysmic variable or 'recurrent nova'. It is a binary system in which a dense burnt-out stellar core – a white dwarf – is pulling gas away from the outer layers of its companion. As the gas collects on the dwarf star, it can reach such temperatures and pressures that it suddenly explodes, causing the system to brighten from magnitude 13 to around magnitude 8 in a few hours, before slowly fading. The star repeats this performance roughly once a month.

Alpha Hydri marks the head of the snake and Beta is two-thirds of the way down the tail. Alpha Hydri is a white star of magnitude 2.9, and lies 78 light years from Earth. Beta is a nearby yellow star of magnitude 2.8, just 21 light years from Earth.

Achernar

VW Hydri

HYDRUS

Indus

Mensa

While Hydra winds its way from east to west across a large region of the sky, Hydrus, the little water snake, zig-zags from north to south, leading the way to the South Celestial Pole. This indistinct constellation was invented by sixteenth-century Dutch navigators Pieter Dirkszoon Keyser and Frederick de Houtman, who were also responsible for a dozen other southern hemisphere constellations. Its pattern is indistinct, but Hydrus is easy to locate because its tail-star lies just southeast of Achernar, the bright star at the end of the long constellation Eridanus.

Indus

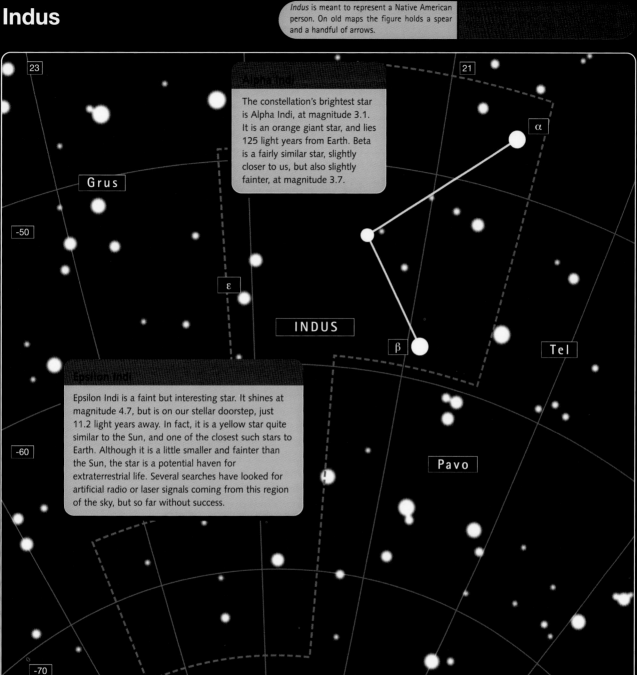

Alpha Indi

The constellation's brightest star is Alpha Indi, at magnitude 3.1. It is an orange giant star, and lies 125 light years from Earth. Beta is a fairly similar star, slightly closer to us, but also slightly fainter, at magnitude 3.7.

Grus

INDUS

Epsilon Indi

Epsilon Indi is a faint but interesting star. It shines at magnitude 4.7, but is on our stellar doorstep, just 11.2 light years away. In fact, it is a yellow star quite similar to the Sun, and one of the closest such stars to Earth. Although it is a little smaller and fainter than the Sun, the star is a potential haven for extraterrestrial life. Several searches have looked for artificial radio or laser signals coming from this region of the sky, but so far without success.

Tel

Pavo

Indus, a southern constellation situated between Pavo and Tucana, was one of 12 constellations introduced by Pieter Dirkszoon Keyser and Frederick De Houtman in the late sixteenth century, and immortalized by Johann Bayer in his 1603 *Uranometria* atlas. Indus is supposed to represent a Native American person. However, its stars are fairly faint and form no recognizable pattern. The constellation is best found looking to the northwest of the Small Magellanic Cloud, which sits nearby like an isolated patch of the Milky Way closer to the South Celestial Pole in Tucana.

Lacerta

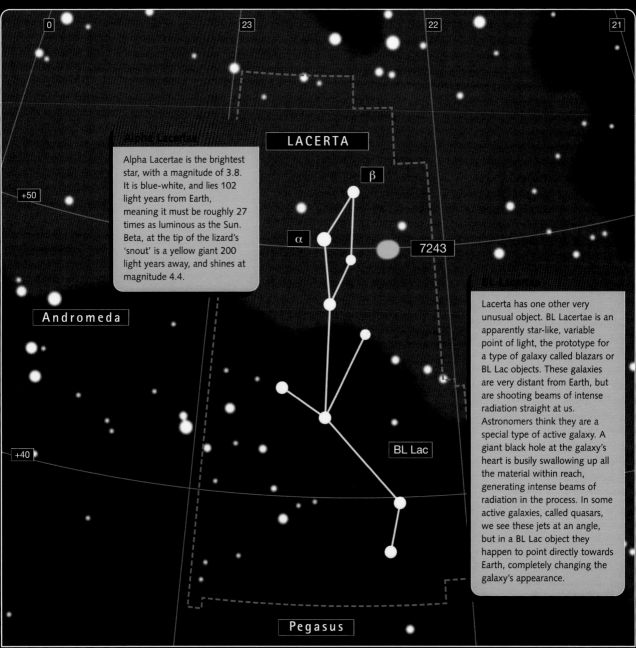

Alpha Lacertae

Alpha Lacertae is the brightest star, with a magnitude of 3.8. It is blue-white, and lies 102 light years from Earth, meaning it must be roughly 27 times as luminous as the Sun. Beta, at the tip of the lizard's 'snout' is a yellow giant 200 light years away, and shines at magnitude 4.4.

BL Lacertae

Lacerta has one other very unusual object. BL Lacertae is an apparently star-like, variable point of light, the prototype for a type of galaxy called blazars or BL Lac objects. These galaxies are very distant from Earth, but are shooting beams of intense radiation straight at us. Astronomers think they are a special type of active galaxy. A giant black hole at the galaxy's heart is busily swallowing up all the material within reach, generating intense beams of radiation in the process. In some active galaxies, called quasars, we see these jets at an angle, but in a BL Lac object they happen to point directly towards Earth, completely changing the galaxy's appearance.

Sitting on the Milky Way between the bright constellations of Cygnus and Cassiopeia, Lacerta is a relatively faint late addition to the constellations of the northern sky. It was invented by Polish astronomer Johannes Hevelius for his *Uranographia* star atlas, published after his death in 1690. The constellation represents a lizard, perhaps suggested by the slithering zig-zag shape of its brighter stars. Although it crosses a dense part of the Milky Way, Lacerta is so small that it contains no bright deep-sky objects. However, the rich star clouds sometimes give rise to nova explosions.

Leo

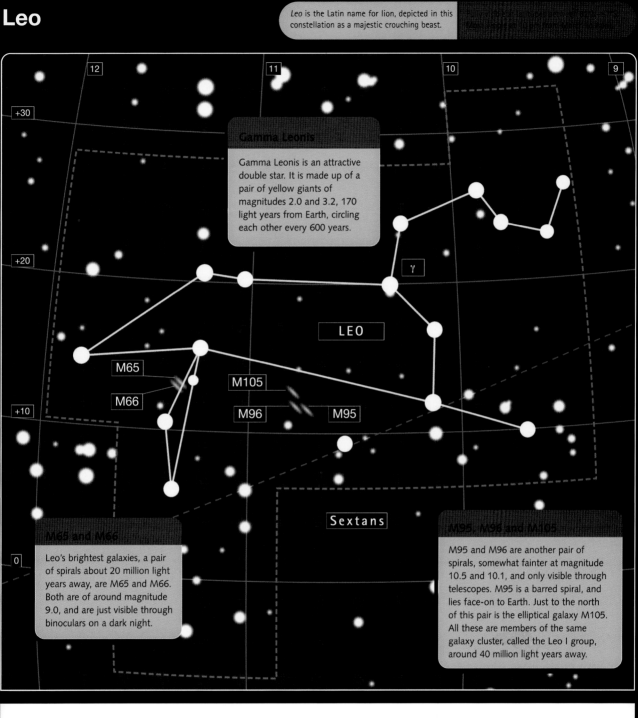

Gamma Leonis

Gamma Leonis is an attractive double star. It is made up of a pair of yellow giants of magnitudes 2.0 and 3.2, 170 light years from Earth, circling each other every 600 years.

LEO

M65

M66

M105

M96

M95

Sextans

M65 and M66

Leo's brightest galaxies, a pair of spirals about 20 million light years away, are M65 and M66. Both are of around magnitude 9.0, and are just visible through binoculars on a dark night.

M95, M96 and M105

M95 and M96 are another pair of spirals, somewhat fainter at magnitude 10.5 and 10.1, and only visible through telescopes. M95 is a barred spiral, and lies face-on to Earth. Just to the north of this pair is the elliptical galaxy M105. All these are members of the same galaxy cluster, called the Leo I group, around 40 million light years away.

Leo is an ancient zodiac constellation, and one of the few that really resemble the figure they are said to represent (in this case, a lion). It is situated between the dim constellation of Cancer to the west and Virgo to the east. Because it lies well away from the Milky Way, it offers some good views of more distant galaxies. It also has an interesting range of stars. In Greek mythology it was identified as the Nemean lion that was killed by Hercules in one of his Twelve Labours, and subsequently placed in the sky. Early Hindu astronomers knew it as Leya or Leyaya, from Leo, as the Romans called it.

Leo Minor

Leo minor translates from the Latin as the lesser lion, here represented as a lion cub.

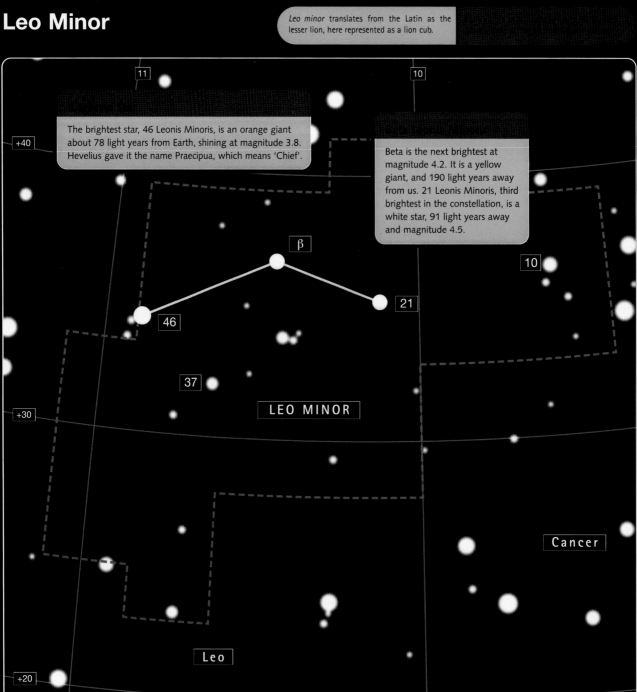

The brightest star, 46 Leonis Minoris, is an orange giant about 78 light years from Earth, shining at magnitude 3.8. Hevelius gave it the name Praecipua, which means 'Chief'.

Beta is the next brightest at magnitude 4.2. It is a yellow giant, and 190 light years away from us. 21 Leonis Minoris, third brightest in the constellation, is a white star, 91 light years away and magnitude 4.5.

LEO MINOR

Cancer

Leo

The faint constellation of Leo Minor, the Little Lion, is situated between Leo and Ursa Major. It was another addition made by Polish astronomer Johannes Hevelius for his systematic catalogue of the skies, the *Uranographia*, in the 1680s. Hevelius claimed that the pattern of stars resembled Leo, which lies directly to the south, but the similarities are certainly not obvious. And, unlike Leo, it does not belong to the ancient list of 48 constellations drawn up by Ptolemy. Leo Minor was ignored or promoted by different astronomers through time, and it survives today almost as an afterthought.

Lepus

Lepus is the Latin name for hare. In this case it is possibly a hare being chased by the great hunter, Orion.

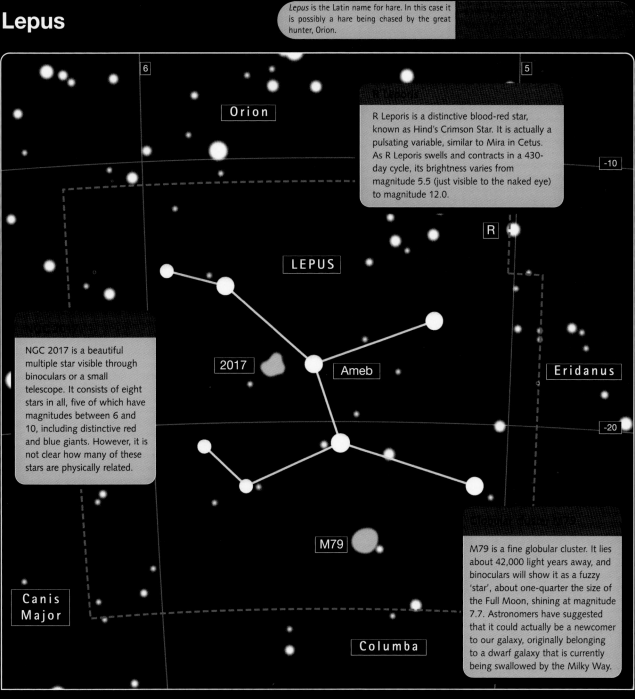

Orion

R Leporis

R Leporis is a distinctive blood-red star, known as Hind's Crimson Star. It is actually a pulsating variable, similar to Mira in Cetus. As R Leporis swells and contracts in a 430-day cycle, its brightness varies from magnitude 5.5 (just visible to the naked eye) to magnitude 12.0.

-10

R

LEPUS

NGC 2017

NGC 2017 is a beautiful multiple star visible through binoculars or a small telescope. It consists of eight stars in all, five of which have magnitudes between 6 and 10, including distinctive red and blue giants. However, it is not clear how many of these stars are physically related.

2017

Ameb

Eridanus

-20

M79

M79

M79 is a fine globular cluster. It lies about 42,000 light years away, and binoculars will show it as a fuzzy 'star', about one-quarter the size of the Full Moon, shining at magnitude 7.7. Astronomers have suggested that it could actually be a newcomer to our galaxy, originally belonging to a dwarf galaxy that is currently being swallowed by the Milky Way.

Canis Major

Columba

This small constellation is easily overlooked because it lies directly to the south of brilliant Orion. It represents a hare crouching at the feet of the great celestial hunter, possibly being chased. The best way to spot the constellation is to look for the distinctive bow-tie shape made by its brighter stars.

The constellation was one of Ptolemy's original 48 and is very old, yet it has little mythology associated with it, apart from being placed in the sky in a position where it could be said to be pursued by Orion. The constellation of Lepus should not be confused with the constellation of Lupus.

Libra

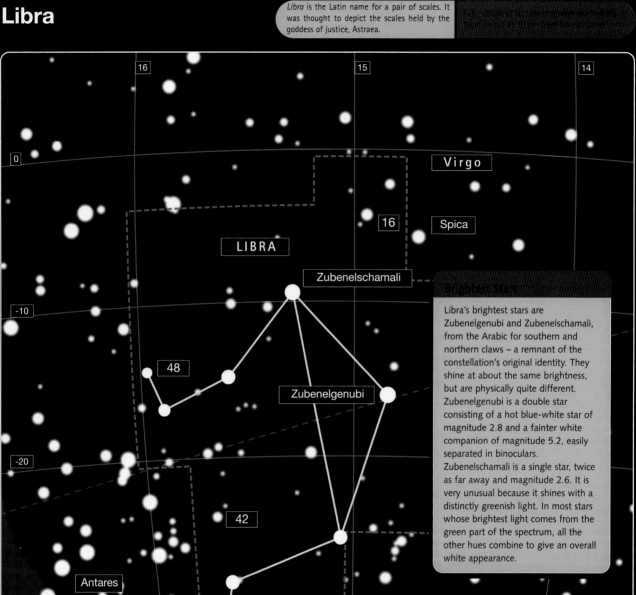

16 15 14

0

Virgo

16

Spica

LIBRA

Zubenelschamali

-10

48

Zubenelgenubi

-20

42

Antares

-30

Lupus

Hydra

Scorpius

Brightest Stars

Libra's brightest stars are Zubenelgenubi and Zubenelschamali, from the Arabic for southern and northern claws – a remnant of the constellation's original identity. They shine at about the same brightness, but are physically quite different. Zubenelgenubi is a double star consisting of a hot blue-white star of magnitude 2.8 and a fainter white companion of magnitude 5.2, easily separated in binoculars. Zubenelschamali is a single star, twice as far away and magnitude 2.6. It is very unusual because it shines with a distinctly greenish light. In most stars whose brightest light comes from the green part of the spectrum, all the other hues combine to give an overall white appearance.

Despite its ancient origin, Libra is a faint and indistinct constellation. However, the area is easily identified because it lies between the bright stars Spica in Virgo and Antares in Scorpius. The constellation of Libra, the scales, is the only sign of the zodiac not named after a living creature. In ancient times, it was known as Chelae Scorpionis, and was said to be the claws of the scorpion (Scorpio, situated next door). Early astronomers (who were also interested in astrology) turned Libra into a separate constellation to even out the amount of time the Sun spent in each part of the zodiac.

Lupus

Libra

16 15 14

-30

2

1

LUPUS

Double and Multiple Stars

Lupus is home to a number of double and multiple stars, including Gamma, Epsilon and Eta. Mu is a nice multiple, with a pair of stars of a magnitude of 4.3 and 7.2 easily separable in a small telescope. More powerful telescopes will show that the brighter star is itself a close double, composed of twin stars of magnitude 5.2.

θ

γ

-40

ε

Norma

μ

-50

NGC 5822

On the southern border of Lupus is NGC 5822, an attractive open cluster of about 150 stars which all formed together in the relatively recent past. It lies about 6000 light years away, and has an overall magnitude around 7.0, making it visible through binoculars. Further north is NGC 5986, a compact and relatively bright globular star cluster, much more distant at 45,000 light years. It shines at magnitude 7, and is visible as a circular blob of light through binoculars or a small telescope.

5822

The constellation of Lupus, the wolf, lies among the bright stars of the southern Milky Way, sandwiched between Scorpius and Centaurus to the south of Libra. Lupus's own stars are fairly bright too, but their pattern is not the most distinct, so the constellation is often lost among its surroundings, yet it was among Ptolemy's original 48 constellations. It has no clear mythology but is sometimes linked with the tale of King Lycaon, a king turned in to a wolf by Zeus because he served him human flesh at a banquet. A later translation of Ptolemy's work identified Lupus as a wolf.

Lynx

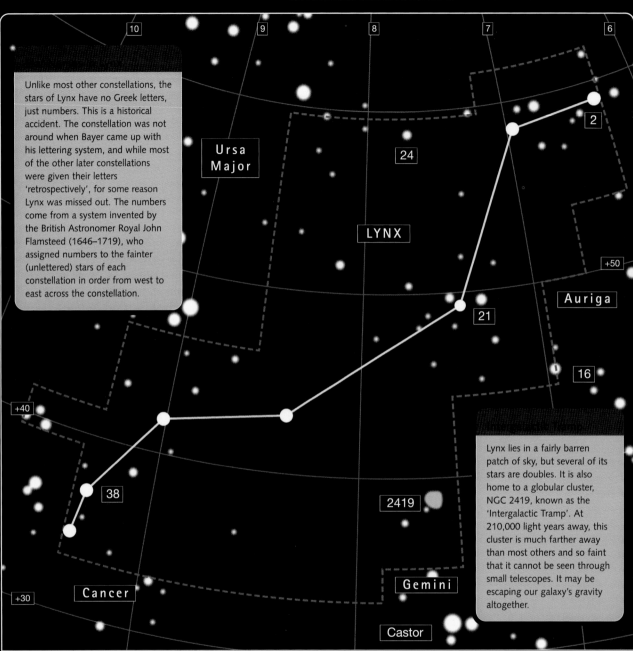

Unlike most other constellations, the stars of Lynx have no Greek letters, just numbers. This is a historical accident. The constellation was not around when Bayer came up with his lettering system, and while most of the other later constellations were given their letters 'retrospectively', for some reason Lynx was missed out. The numbers come from a system invented by the British Astronomer Royal John Flamsteed (1646–1719), who assigned numbers to the fainter (unlettered) stars of each constellation in order from west to east across the constellation.

Lynx lies in a fairly barren patch of sky, but several of its stars are doubles. It is also home to a globular cluster, NGC 2419, known as the 'Intergalactic Tramp'. At 210,000 light years away, this cluster is much farther away than most others and so faint that it cannot be seen through small telescopes. It may be escaping our galaxy's gravity altogether.

The constellation of Lynx (named for a type of wild cat) is another late addition to northern skies. It is unexpectedly large, greater in area than, for example, Gemini. It was invented in the late seventeenth century by the great mapper of stars, Johannes Hevelius (also responsible for Lacerta and Leo Minor). Lynx separates the 'forepaws' of the Great Bear, Ursa Major, from the stars of Auriga, the Charioteer. Hevelius came up with the name as a joke. He thought the long chain of stars was so faint that only those with the eyesight of a lynx would be able to see it.

Lyra

20 19 18 +50

Draco

Epsilon Lyrae is a beautiful 'double-double' star system, 160 light years away. Binoculars will easily show the system as two stars of magnitudes 6.0 and 5.2, but each of these is itself a double that can be seen through a small telescope.

Vega (Alpha Lyrae) is the fifth-brightest star in the whole sky, at magnitude 0.0. It is 25 light years from Earth, and is surrounded by a ring of dust and gas, which may be forming planets.

R

LYRA

+40

ε   Vega

Cygnus

Hercules

β

+30

M57

Beta Lyrae is also a multiple star. Binoculars will show a bright yellow-white star with a magnitude 7.2 white companion, but the brighter star is also a double, too close to separate through even the most powerful telescopes. Its nature is revealed by periodic and sudden dips in its brightness, as one star passes in front of the other and the total amount of light reaching us from the system is reduced. Astronomers call this kind of system an 'eclipsing binary'.

M57 is the delicate and beautiful Ring Nebula, a planetary nebula 1,100 light years away. This is a spherical shell of gas puffed off by a dying star, and shines at magnitude 9.7, making it a good object for small telescopes.

Hercules

The constellation of Lyra figures prominently in the northern skies between Cygnus and Hercules. It is named after the lyre, an ancient musical instrument that features in the Greek legend of Orpheus in the Underworld. According to mythology, Orpheus was even able to charm Hades with the sweet music of his lyre, and the instrument was placed in the stars upon his death. Arab astronomers saw Lyra as a swooping eagle, which is where Lyra's star, Vega, one of the brightest stars in the sky, gets its name. Earlier the constellation was seen as a vulture and later a vulture playing a lyre.

Mensa

Stars in Mensa

Unfortunately, none of the stars in Mensa are particularly noteworthy. Alpha is a decidedly average, sun-like yellow star, 30 light years from Earth and shining at magnitude 5.1. Beta makes an interesting comparison because it is also yellow, and just slightly fainter at magnitude 5.3. But its distance is about 300 light years, meaning that this star is actually a yellow giant nearing the end of its life and on the way to becoming a red giant. Because of the way light spreads out the farther on it travels from a star, astronomers can guess that Beta, ten times farther away than Alpha, must be 100 times more luminous in order to shine with the same magnitude on Earth.

Mensa is another of the faint and generally dull constellations introduced to the southern skies by Nicolas Louis de Lacaille in the middle of the eighteenth century. when he was surveying the stars in Cape Town. Mensa, whose name means 'table' in Latin, was named after nearby Table Mountain, which overlooks the city. It may qualify as the faintest constellation in the sky: none of its stars is brighter than magnitude 5.0. It is fairly easy to locate under dark southern skies, however, because it sits between the South Celestial Pole and the Large Magellanic Cloud (LMC).

Microscopium

Microscopium is the Latin for microscope and is one of the constellations that Nicolas Louis de La Caille named after scientific instruments.

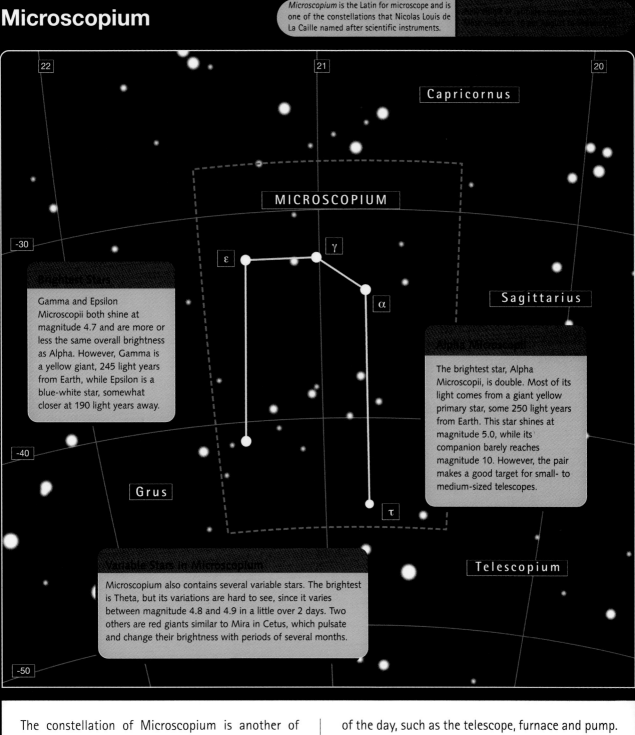

Brightest Stars

Gamma and Epsilon Microscopii both shine at magnitude 4.7 and are more or less the same overall brightness as Alpha. However, Gamma is a yellow giant, 245 light years from Earth, while Epsilon is a blue-white star, somewhat closer at 190 light years away.

Alpha Microscopii

The brightest star, Alpha Microscopii, is double. Most of its light comes from a giant yellow primary star, some 250 light years from Earth. This star shines at magnitude 5.0, while its companion barely reaches magnitude 10. However, the pair makes a good target for small- to medium-sized telescopes.

Variable Stars in Microscopium

Microscopium also contains several variable stars. The brightest is Theta, but its variations are hard to see, since it varies between magnitude 4.8 and 4.9 in a little over 2 days. Two others are red giants similar to Mira in Cetus, which pulsate and change their brightness with periods of several months.

The constellation of Microscopium is another of Lacaille's southern-hemisphere inventions of the 1750s and it is supposed to represent a microscope, though in reality it bears no relation whatsoever to the scientific instrument. It is one of a group of constellations De La Caille named after instruments of the day, such as the telescope, furnace and pump. A fairly shapeless scattering of faint stars, it is situated between the brighter stars of Piscis Austrinus and Sagittarius. It contains only 4th magnitude or fainter stars and has no major deep-sky objects.

Monoceros

The name *Monoceros* is Greek for unicorn, the mythical horse with one horn on its forehead. It is a symbol of chastity and purity.

+10
0
Cancer
MONOCEROS
Orion
Canis Major
2264
S
2237
2244
β
M50
α
8
7
6

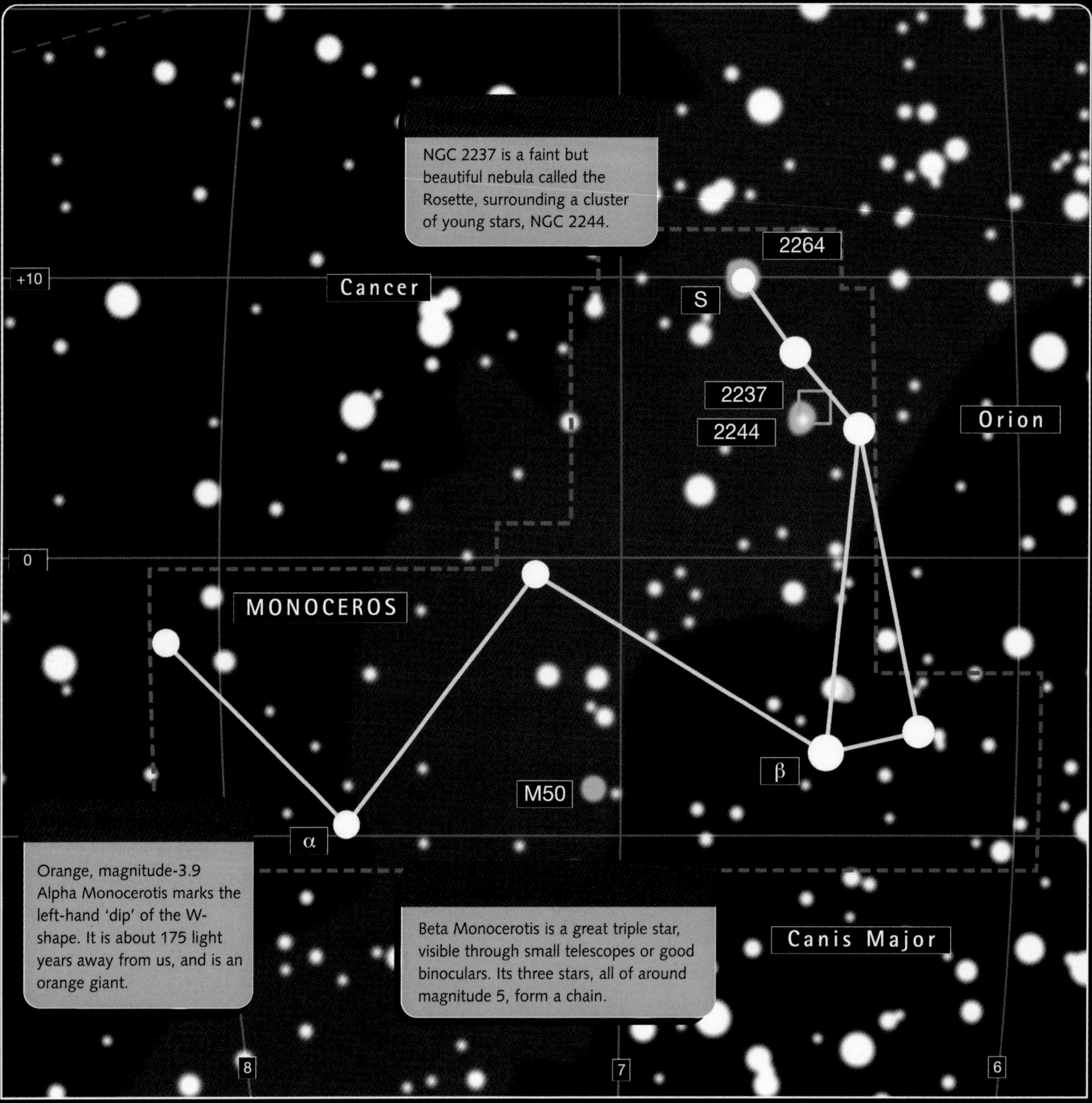

NGC 2237 is a faint but beautiful nebula called the Rosette, surrounding a cluster of young stars, NGC 2244.

Orange, magnitude-3.9 Alpha Monocerotis marks the left-hand 'dip' of the W-shape. It is about 175 light years away from us, and is an orange giant.

Beta Monocerotis is a great triple star, visible through small telescopes or good binoculars. Its three stars, all of around magnitude 5, form a chain.

A modern constellation, Monoceros is believed to have been named by the Dutch astronomer and theologian Petrus Plancius in 1613. It may well predate this, however, as it has been found portrayed on a ancient Persian sphere. The stars of Monoceros, the Unicorn, form a wide 'W' in the skies directly east of Orion. They are faint compared to the many of the constellations nearby, but Monoceros has other attractions. It is crossed by a rich strip of the Milky Way – part of the spiral arm closest to our Solar System – and boasts several attractive star clusters and nebulae.

Musca

The name *Musca* is the Latin word for a fly.

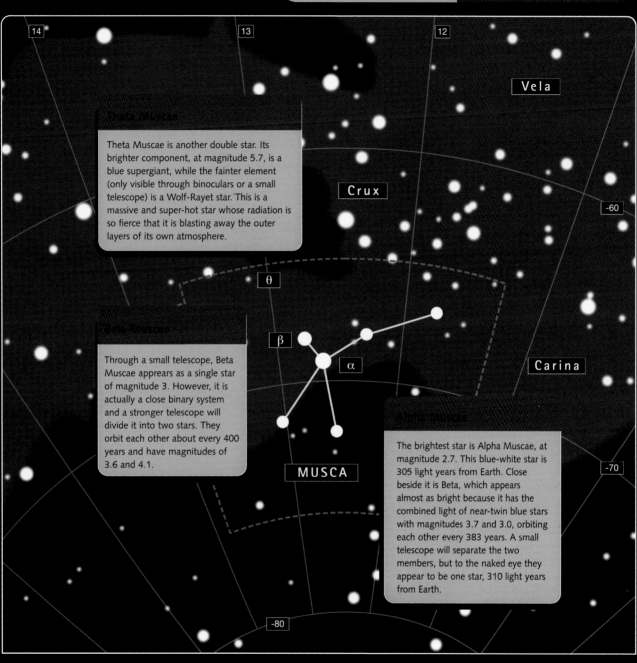

Theta Muscae

Theta Muscae is another double star. Its brighter component, at magnitude 5.7, is a blue supergiant, while the fainter element (only visible through binoculars or a small telescope) is a Wolf-Rayet star. This is a massive and super-hot star whose radiation is so fierce that it is blasting away the outer layers of its own atmosphere.

Beta Muscae

Through a small telescope, Beta Muscae apprears as a single star of magnitude 3. However, it is actually a close binary system and a stronger telescope will divide it into two stars. They orbit each other about every 400 years and have magnitudes of 3.6 and 4.1.

Alpha Muscae

The brightest star is Alpha Muscae, at magnitude 2.7. This blue-white star is 305 light years from Earth. Close beside it is Beta, which appears almost as bright because it has the combined light of near-twin blue stars with magnitudes 3.7 and 3.0, orbiting each other every 383 years. A small telescope will separate the two members, but to the naked eye they appear to be one star, 310 light years from Earth.

Vela

Crux

Carina

MUSCA

Of the dozen constellations invented by Dutch explorers Pieter Dirkszoon Keyser and Frederick De Houtman in the late 1500s, Musca is probably the most distinctive. Its stars are relatively bright, it lies in the Milky Way and it happens to be situated directly between the really bright stars of Crux and the South Celestial Pole. Because the constellation Musca was only introduced by Johann Bayer in his star atlas *Uranometria* as recently as 1603 and lies near the southern pole, Musca was not known to classical or early cultures. As a result, there is no early mythology associated with it.

Norma

The name *Norma* is Latin for normal, meaning right angle. This constellation is also called The Rule, Carpenter's Square, Set Square or Level.

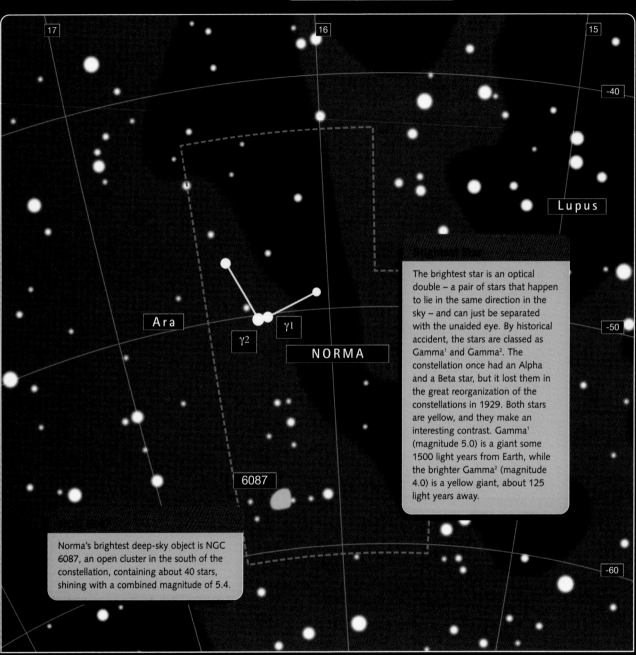

Lupus

Ara

γ2

γ1

NORMA

6087

Brightest Star

The brightest star is an optical double – a pair of stars that happen to lie in the same direction in the sky – and can just be separated with the unaided eye. By historical accident, the stars are classed as Gamma[1] and Gamma[2]. The constellation once had an Alpha and a Beta star, but it lost them in the great reorganization of the constellations in 1929. Both stars are yellow, and they make an interesting contrast. Gamma[1] (magnitude 5.0) is a giant some 1500 light years from Earth, while the brighter Gamma[2] (magnitude 4.0) is a yellow giant, about 125 light years away.

Norma's brightest deep-sky object is NGC 6087, an open cluster in the south of the constellation, containing about 40 stars, shining with a combined magnitude of 5.4.

Norma is a small and inconspicuous collection of indistinct stars in the southern hemisphere, situated between Scorpius and Lupus. It was named by Nicolas Louis de Lacaille in the eighteenth century during his stay at the Cape of Good Hope from 1751 to 1752. The constellation is supposed to represent a level (a measuring instrument used by surveyors), though originally de Lacaille called it Norma et Regula (The Set Square and The Ruler), in reference to the tools used by carpenters. The constellation had previously been called Euclid's Square. There is no early or classical mythology associated with it.

Octans

Octans is the Latin name for the octant, an instrument used for observing altitudes of a celestial body from a moving ship.

Fully visible at latitudes between 0°N–90°S.
Most visible at 10 pm in October.

23   22   21   20   19

Indus

Pavo

-70

γ

α

β

OCTANS

-80

Hydrus

σ

South
celestial pole

δ

Delta Octantis

Delta is an orange giant star, 185 light years from Earth, and visible at magnitude 4.3. Beta, Gamma and Delta are all strangely brighter than Alpha. This is likely due to a mistake by Lacaille rather than an actual change in the brightness of the stars. Alpha itself is a yellow-white star of magnitude 5.2, 390 light years away. By studying the way its light behaves, astronomers have discovered that it is actually a binary star even though the two components are far too close to separate from Earth.

Sigma Octantis

Sigma Octantis is an average white star of magnitude 5.4, about 300 light years away. It is only noteworthy because it is the naked-eye star closest to the South Celestial Pole, and so is the southern pole star. Through the course of a day and a night, the southern heavens appear to spin around this one fixed point in the sky.

Octans is the southern sky's equivalent of Ursa Minor, the Little Bear. It is mainly significant in that it contains the South Celestial Pole, and is therefore visible all night from all across the southern hemisphere, slowly rotating once every 24 hours.

Unfortunately, Octans is an uninspiring region of the sky. The constellation is another of Lacaille's eighteenth-century inventions, and represents a type of navigational instrument called an octant, a predecessor of the sextant. There is no classical or early mythology associated with this constellation because it was not visible in the Mediterranean.

Ophiuchus

Ophiuchus represents Asclepius, the Greek god of medicine, holding the snake from whom he learned the secrets of life and death.

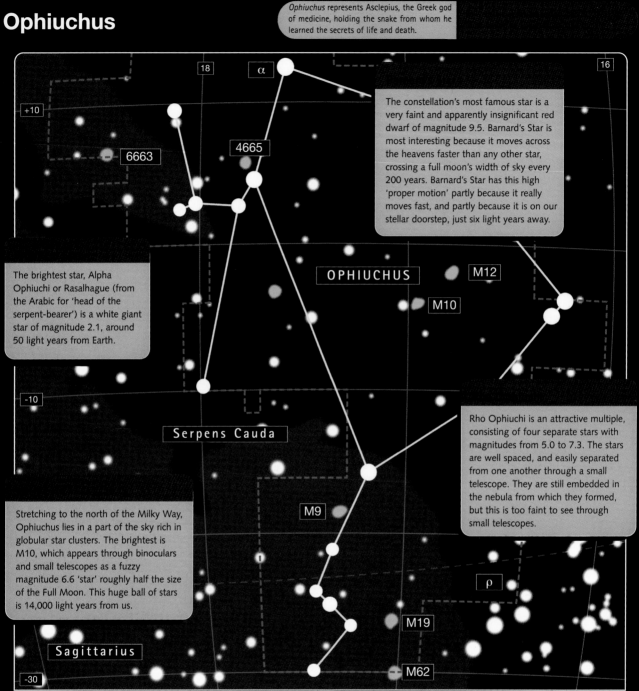

The constellation's most famous star is a very faint and apparently insignificant red dwarf of magnitude 9.5. Barnard's Star is most interesting because it moves across the heavens faster than any other star, crossing a full moon's width of sky every 200 years. Barnard's Star has this high 'proper motion' partly because it really moves fast, and partly because it is on our stellar doorstep, just six light years away.

The brightest star, Alpha Ophiuchi or Rasalhague (from the Arabic for 'head of the serpent-bearer') is a white giant star of magnitude 2.1, around 50 light years from Earth.

Rho Ophiuchi is an attractive multiple, consisting of four separate stars with magnitudes from 5.0 to 7.3. The stars are well spaced, and easily separated from one another through a small telescope. They are still embedded in the nebula from which they formed, but this is too faint to see through small telescopes.

Stretching to the north of the Milky Way, Ophiuchus lies in a part of the sky rich in globular star clusters. The brightest is M10, which appears through binoculars and small telescopes as a fuzzy magnitude 6.6 'star' roughly half the size of the Full Moon. This huge ball of stars is 14,000 light years from us.

Ophiuchus is large and well spaced out constellation, but its stars are also relatively faint, so the pattern can be hard to identify. This ancient constellation is known in English as the Serpent-bearer. It represents a figure, the physician Asclepius, wrestling a snake (the constellation Serpens). Asclepius had learnt the secrets of life and death from watching one serpent bring herbs to another. In order to stop the human race from becoming immortal under Asclepius's care, Zeus eventually killed him with a bolt of lightning, but placed him in the skies in honour of his good works.

Orion

Orion is the name of the son of Poseidon. He is depicted as a hunter who is fighting Taurus the bull with his dogs Canis Major and Canis Minor.

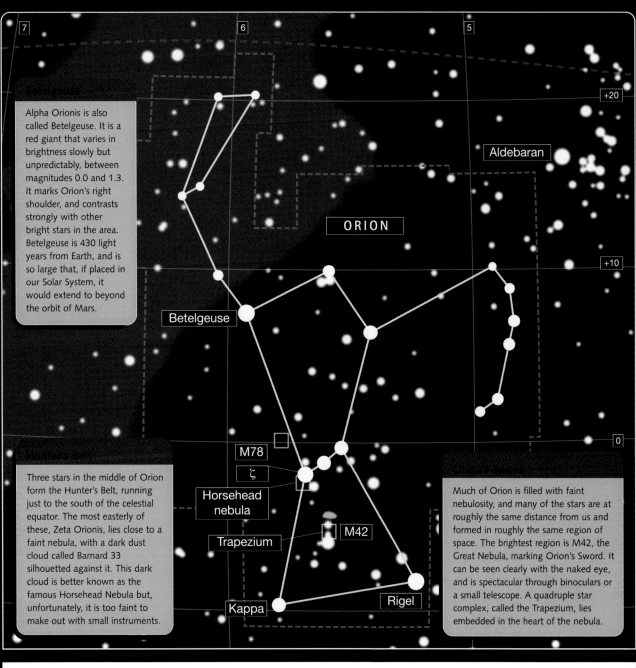

Betelgeuse

Alpha Orionis is also called Betelgeuse. It is a red giant that varies in brightness slowly but unpredictably, between magnitudes 0.0 and 1.3. It marks Orion's right shoulder, and contrasts strongly with other bright stars in the area. Betelgeuse is 430 light years from Earth, and is so large that, if placed in our Solar System, it would extend to beyond the orbit of Mars.

Hunter's Belt

Three stars in the middle of Orion form the Hunter's Belt, running just to the south of the celestial equator. The most easterly of these, Zeta Orionis, lies close to a faint nebula, with a dark dust cloud called Barnard 33 silhouetted against it. This dark cloud is better known as the famous Horsehead Nebula but, unfortunately, it is too faint to make out with small instruments.

Orion's Sword

Much of Orion is filled with faint nebulosity, and many of the stars are at roughly the same distance from us and formed in roughly the same region of space. The brightest region is M42, the Great Nebula, marking Orion's Sword. It can be seen clearly with the naked eye, and is spectacular through binoculars or a small telescope. A quadruple star complex, called the Trapezium, lies embedded in the heart of the nebula.

One of the brightest, most prominent and easily recognized constellations in the sky, Orion is rich in bright stars and star-forming nebula regions. The figure of Orion is depicted standing by the River Eridanus with his two hunting dogs, fighting Taurus the bull. Other prey, such as Lepus, the hare, are situated nearby. In one story, Orion was accidentally shot and killed by the hunting goddess, Diana, who then placed him in the sky to commemorate him. In another myth, Orion, the son of Poseidon, was bitten by a scorpion and died. As Orion sets in the night sky, the constellation Scorpius rises.

Pavo

Alpha and Beta Pavonis

The blue-white star Alpha Pavonis is itself known as 'The Peacock'. It is 360 light years away, and shines at magnitude 1.9, clearly marking the constellation's northeastern corner. The next brightest star, Beta, is white, magnitude 3.4 and about 88 light years away.

NGC 6752

NGC 6752 is a globular cluster of stars in orbit around the Milky Way. It lies relatively close for a globular cluster (14,000 light years away), and shines at about magnitude 5. Just to its south lies NGC 6744, a face-on barred spiral galaxy whose bright central regions can be seen through a small telescope, shining at around magnitude 9.

Ara

Indus

6752

PAVO

α

β

κ

Octans

Kappa Pavonis

Kappa Pavonis is a Cepheid variable star. This means that it is a yellow supergiant, passing through an unstable phase of its life where it pulsates, expanding and contracting every few days, and changing its brightness as it does so. Kappa is actually one of the brightest Cepheids in the sky. It varies between magnitude 3.9 and 4.8 in a cycle that repeats every 9.1 days.

When Dutch navigators Pieter Dirkszoon Keyser and Frederick de Houtman were creating constellations in the late 1500s they used birds for several of them. The constellation Pavo, the peacock, is one such example. It is a large constellation supposedly depicting the fully opened tail of a peacock, and it lies in a fairly barren area of sky. However, it is marked by one particularly bright star and has a few deep-sky objects. Because the constellation was only created in the 17th century and was not visible in the Mediterranean, there is no classical or Greek mythology associated with Pavo.

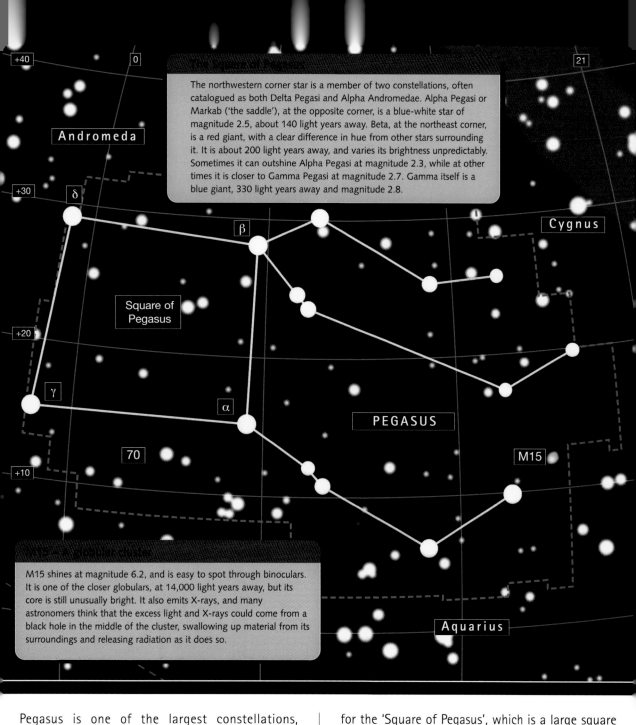

The Square of Pegasus

The northwestern corner star is a member of two constellations, often catalogued as both Delta Pegasi and Alpha Andromedae. Alpha Pegasi or Markab ('the saddle'), at the opposite corner, is a blue-white star of magnitude 2.5, about 140 light years away. Beta, at the northeast corner, is a red giant, with a clear difference in hue from other stars surrounding it. It is about 200 light years away, and varies its brightness unpredictably. Sometimes it can outshine Alpha Pegasi at magnitude 2.3, while at other times it is closer to Gamma Pegasi at magnitude 2.7. Gamma itself is a blue giant, 330 light years away and magnitude 2.8.

Andromeda

Cygnus

+30   δ

β

Square of Pegasus

+20

γ

α

PEGASUS

70

M15

+10

M15 – A globular cluster

M15 shines at magnitude 6.2, and is easy to spot through binoculars. It is one of the closer globulars, at 14,000 light years away, but its core is still unusually bright. It also emits X-rays, and many astronomers think that the excess light and X-rays could come from a black hole in the middle of the cluster, swallowing up material from its surroundings and releasing radiation as it does so.

Aquarius

Pegasus is one of the largest constellations, encompassing a huge and somewhat empty region of the sky. Although this constellation contains relatively few deep-sky objects, and lies some distance from the Milky Way, it does have one bright globular cluster. It is easy to spot by looking for the 'Square of Pegasus', which is a large square of sky with its corners marked by four stars of roughly equal brightness. According to Greek myth, Hercules had to steal one of the four wild mares. Bucephalus, Alexander the Great's horse, was also said to have been descended from these mares.

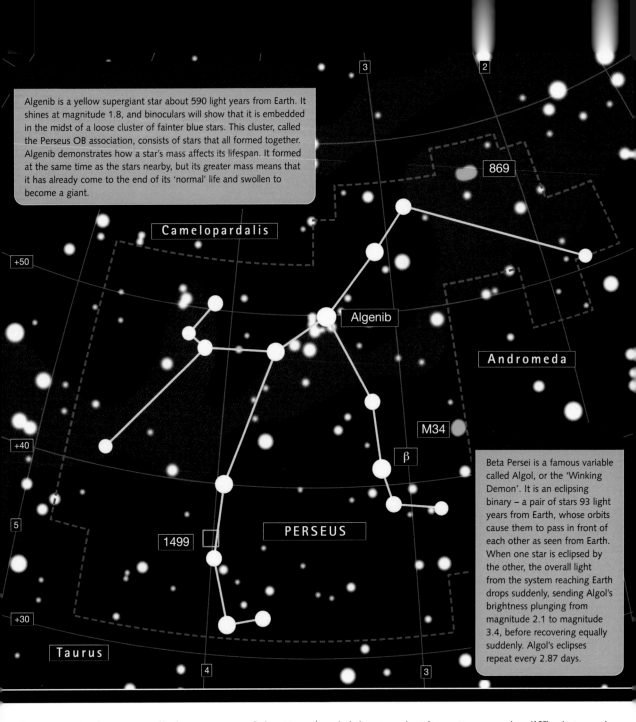

Algenib is a yellow supergiant star about 590 light years from Earth. It shines at magnitude 1.8, and binoculars will show that it is embedded in the midst of a loose cluster of fainter blue stars. This cluster, called the Perseus OB association, consists of stars that all formed together. Algenib demonstrates how a star's mass affects its lifespan. It formed at the same time as the stars nearby, but its greater mass means that it has already come to the end of its 'normal' life and swollen to become a giant.

3

2

869

Camelopardalis

+50

Algenib

Andromeda

+40

M34

β

5

PERSEUS

1499

Beta Persei is a famous variable called Algol, or the 'Winking Demon'. It is an eclipsing binary – a pair of stars 93 light years from Earth, whose orbits cause them to pass in front of each other as seen from Earth. When one star is eclipsed by the other, the overall light from the system reaching Earth drops suddenly, sending Algol's brightness plunging from magnitude 2.1 to magnitude 3.4, before recovering equally suddenly. Algol's eclipses repeat every 2.87 days.

+30

Taurus

4

3

Perseus, a northern constellation, was one of the 48 constellations named by Ptolemy. It is very bright and represents the Greek hero of a myth that links the surrounding constellations including Andromeda, Cassiopeia, Cepheus and Cetus. Perseus lies in a dense region of the Milky Way, and contains many bright stars, but its pattern can be difficult to make out. Beta Persei (*see above*) famously represents the eye of the gorgon Medusa, whose gaze could turn anyone to stone. According to the mythology, Perseus cut off Medusa's head, and used it to turn the sea monster Cetus to stone.

Phoenix

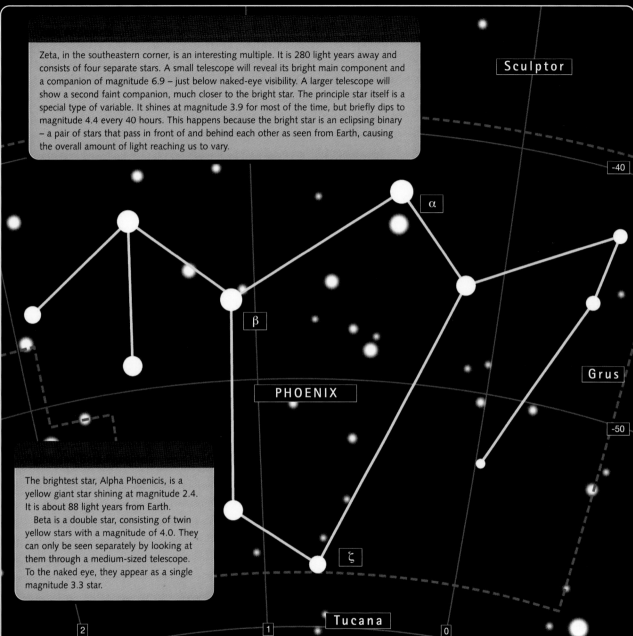

Zeta, in the southeastern corner, is an interesting multiple. It is 280 light years away and consists of four separate stars. A small telescope will reveal its bright main component and a companion of magnitude 6.9 – just below naked-eye visibility. A larger telescope will show a second faint companion, much closer to the bright star. The principle star itself is a special type of variable. It shines at magnitude 3.9 for most of the time, but briefly dips to magnitude 4.4 every 40 hours. This happens because the bright star is an eclipsing binary – a pair of stars that pass in front of and behind each other as seen from Earth, causing the overall amount of light reaching us to vary.

Sculptor

α

-40

β

Grus

PHOENIX

-50

The brightest star, Alpha Phoenicis, is a yellow giant star shining at magnitude 2.4. It is about 88 light years from Earth.
Beta is a double star, consisting of twin yellow stars with a magnitude of 4.0. They can only be seen separately by looking at them through a medium-sized telescope. To the naked eye, they appear as a single magnitude 3.3 star.

ζ

Tucana

2   1   0

The constellation of Phoenix represents the mythological firebird that regenerates itself from its own ashes, or, in other stories, rises from the dead body of its predecessor. It is one of several birds added to the southern sky by Dutch explorers Pieter Dirkszoon Keyser and Frederick de Houtman in the late 1500s. The constellation's shape is fairly indistinct, but it is easily found because it lies directly to the west of Achernar, the star at the end of the River Eridanus. In ancient times, Arab astronomers called this same group of stars Al Zaurak – a boat moored to the bank of Eridanus.

Pictor

Pictor is the Latin name for a painter's easel.

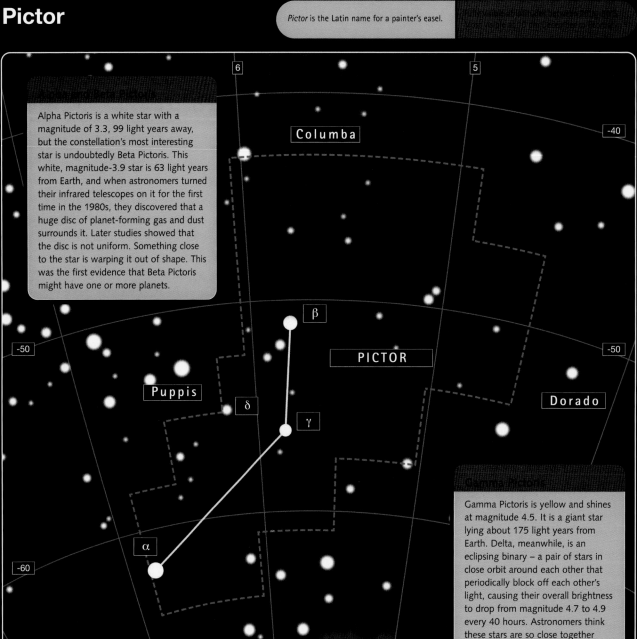

Alpha Pictoris is a white star with a magnitude of 3.3, 99 light years away, but the constellation's most interesting star is undoubtedly Beta Pictoris. This white, magnitude-3.9 star is 63 light years from Earth, and when astronomers turned their infrared telescopes on it for the first time in the 1980s, they discovered that a huge disc of planet-forming gas and dust surrounds it. Later studies showed that the disc is not uniform. Something close to the star is warping it out of shape. This was the first evidence that Beta Pictoris might have one or more planets.

Gamma Pictoris is yellow and shines at magnitude 4.5. It is a giant star lying about 175 light years from Earth. Delta, meanwhile, is an eclipsing binary – a pair of stars in close orbit around each other that periodically block off each other's light, causing their overall brightness to drop from magnitude 4.7 to 4.9 every 40 hours. Astronomers think these stars are so close together that they are actually pulled into egg shapes by each other's gravity.

Pictor is another fairly faint southern constellation, invented by Nicolas Louis de Lacaille in the middle of the 18th century to fill empty space that was not visible to the Greeks. In this case, the constellation is supposed to represent a painter's easel, and it is one of the instruments of arts and science that de Lacaille turned into constellations. Although it lacks a distinct pattern, Pictor is still fairly easy to identify because of its position just to the west of Canopus, the second-brightest star in the sky, and east of the Large Magellanic Cloud. There is no early mythology surrounding this constellation.

Pisces

Pisces is the Latin word for fish. In Greek mythology, these fish were Aphrodite and Eros in disguise, fleeing the monster Typhon.

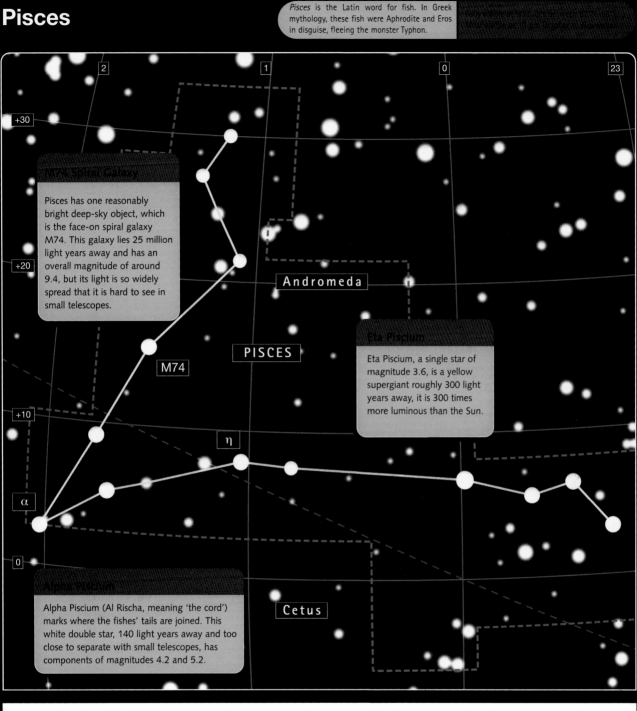

M74 Spiral Galaxy

Pisces has one reasonably bright deep-sky object, which is the face-on spiral galaxy M74. This galaxy lies 25 million light years away and has an overall magnitude of around 9.4, but its light is so widely spread that it is hard to see in small telescopes.

Andromeda

PISCES

Eta Piscium

Eta Piscium, a single star of magnitude 3.6, is a yellow supergiant roughly 300 light years away, it is 300 times more luminous than the Sun.

M74

η

α

Cetus

Alpha Piscium

Alpha Piscium (Al Rischa, meaning 'the cord') marks where the fishes' tails are joined. This white double star, 140 light years away and too close to separate with small telescopes, has components of magnitudes 4.2 and 5.2.

The stars of Pisces are faint, and its pattern difficult to make out, yet astronomers since ancient times have seen Pisces as a pair of fish, their tails entwined. It is a zodiacal constellation, and the Sun, Moon and planets are frequently found here. In fact, Pisces is currently the most important zodiac constellation, as this is where the Sun crosses the celestial equator at the start of northern spring. This location (known confusingly as the First Point of Aries) lies almost exactly south of Omega Piscium and marks the point from which all celestial coordinates are measured.

Piscis Austrinus

Piscis Austrinis is the Latin term for southern fish. The fish here is depicted as having water poured into its mouth by Aquarius.

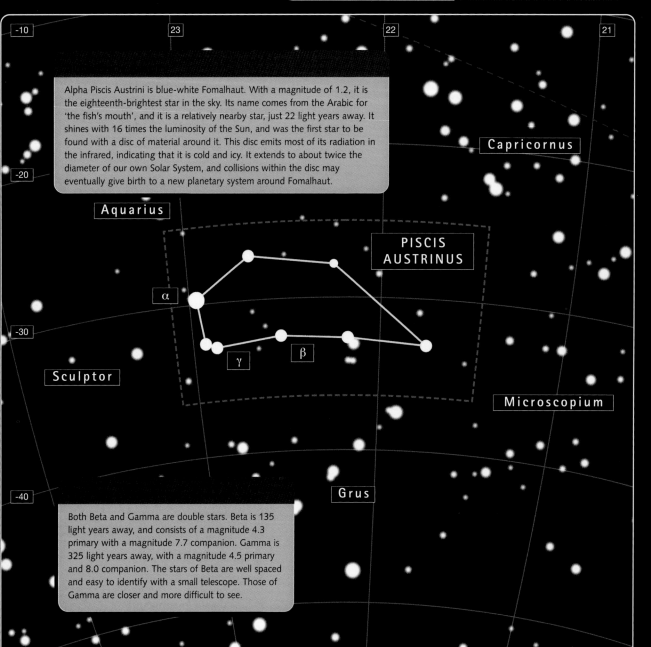

-10 **23** **22** **21**

Alpha Piscis Austrini is blue-white Fomalhaut. With a magnitude of 1.2, it is the eighteenth-brightest star in the sky. Its name comes from the Arabic for 'the fish's mouth', and it is a relatively nearby star, just 22 light years away. It shines with 16 times the luminosity of the Sun, and was the first star to be found with a disc of material around it. This disc emits most of its radiation in the infrared, indicating that it is cold and icy. It extends to about twice the diameter of our own Solar System, and collisions within the disc may eventually give birth to a new planetary system around Fomalhaut.

Capricornus

-20

Aquarius

PISCIS AUSTRINUS

α

-30

γ

β

Sculptor

Microscopium

-40

Grus

Both Beta and Gamma are double stars. Beta is 135 light years away, and consists of a magnitude 4.3 primary with a magnitude 7.7 companion. Gamma is 325 light years away, with a magnitude 4.5 primary and 8.0 companion. The stars of Beta are well spaced and easy to identify with a small telescope. Those of Gamma are closer and more difficult to see.

Although it contains just one bright star, Piscis Austrinus, the Southern Fish, was one of the original 48 constellations immortalized by Ptolemy. It was supposed to be a fish lying on its back drinking in the flow of water being poured out of the jars of nearby Aquarius. The twin fishes of Pisces were said to be its offspring because originally Piscis Austrinus was the only constellation thought to be a fish. The Arabs called the constellation Al Hut al Janubiyy (the Large Southern Fish). It is also believed that the constellation referred to the Assyrian fish god, Dagon, and the Babylonian god, Oannes.

Puppis

Puppis is the Latin name for the poop deck of a ship. Puppis is one of the parts of *Argo Navis*, the ship of Jason and the Argonauts.

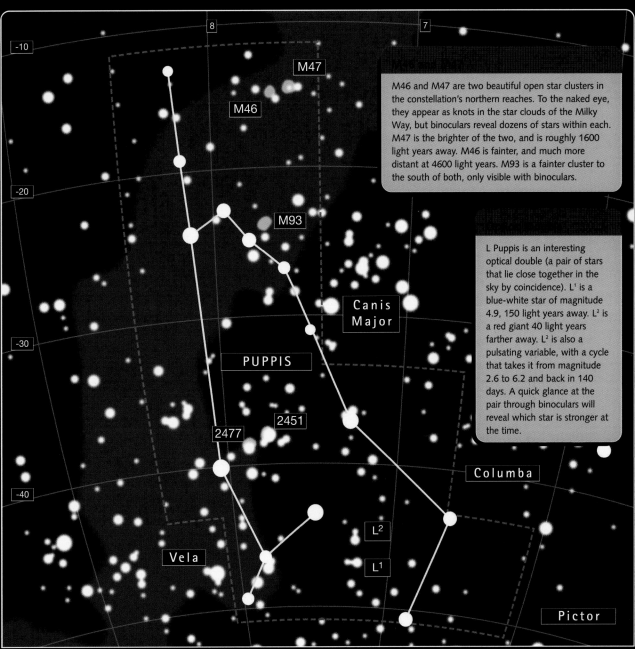

M46 and M47

M46 and M47 are two beautiful open star clusters in the constellation's northern reaches. To the naked eye, they appear as knots in the star clouds of the Milky Way, but binoculars reveal dozens of stars within each. M47 is the brighter of the two, and is roughly 1600 light years away. M46 is fainter, and much more distant at 4600 light years. M93 is a fainter cluster to the south of both, only visible with binoculars.

L Puppis is an interesting optical double (a pair of stars that lie close together in the sky by coincidence). L¹ is a blue-white star of magnitude 4.9, 150 light years away. L² is a red giant 40 light years farther away. L² is also a pulsating variable, with a cycle that takes it from magnitude 2.6 to 6.2 and back in 140 days. A quick glance at the pair through binoculars will reveal which star is stronger at the time.

Puppis, along with its companions Vela and Carina, was once part of the largest constellation in the sky – the great ship *Argo Navis* of Greek mythology. Puppis, the largest part, represents the stern of the vessel, and has been around since ancient times. The current constellation lies in a particularly crowded area of the sky. It is crossed by dense Milky Way starfields, and contains several interesting deep-sky objects. Since Puppis was once part of a larger constellation it has no stars labelled alpha (α), beta (β), gamma (γ), delta (δ) or epsilon (ε), nor is there any early mythology specifically about Puppis.

Pyxis

Pyxis is the Latin name for compass.

Fully visible at latitudes between 52°N–80°S
Most visible at 10 pm February to March.

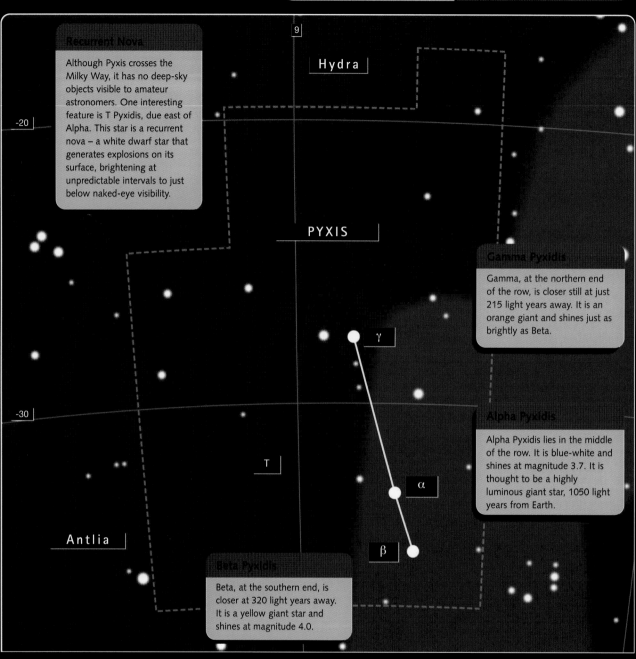

9

Hydra

-20

Recurrent Nova

Although Pyxis crosses the Milky Way, it has no deep-sky objects visible to amateur astronomers. One interesting feature is T Pyxidis, due east of Alpha. This star is a recurrent nova – a white dwarf star that generates explosions on its surface, brightening at unpredictable intervals to just below naked-eye visibility.

PYXIS

Gamma Pyxidis

Gamma, at the northern end of the row, is closer still at just 215 light years away. It is an orange giant and shines just as brightly as Beta.

γ

-30

Alpha Pyxidis

Alpha Pyxidis lies in the middle of the row. It is blue-white and shines at magnitude 3.7. It is thought to be a highly luminous giant star, 1050 light years from Earth.

T

α

Antlia

β

Beta Pyxidis

Beta, at the southern end, is closer at 320 light years away. It is a yellow giant star and shines at magnitude 4.0.

This southern constellation is situated on the edge of the Milky Way. The stars of Pyxis are meant to represent a magnetic compass, another invention of the French astronomer Nicolas Louis de Lacaille from the middle of the 18th century. Appropriately, he placed his new constellation next to the stars of the great ship *Argo Navis*. Pyxis lies just to the east of Puppis, the stern, and to the north of Vela, the sails. As with many of Lacaille's constellations, Pyxis is fairly indistinct. Its pattern is simply three bright stars in a row (in antiquity, they may have been seen as part of *Argo*'s mast).

Reticulum

Reticulum is the Latin name for a device known as a grid or reticle, used in the eyepiece of a telescope for recording star positions.

5

4

3

-50

Brightest Star

The constellation is small and sits in a fairly barren part of the sky, so it has no deep-sky objects of note. The brightest star, Alpha Reticuli, is a yellow giant 135 light years from Earth, and shines at magnitude 3.4.

Beta Reticuli

The next brightest is Beta Reticuli at magnitude 3.9. It is an orange star 78 light years away. Gamma, the star in the middle of the reticule, is a red giant with a magnitude of 4.5, 490 light years distant.

Dorado

Horologium

RETICULUM

-60

ζ^2

Zeta Reticuli

A little to the west of the main constellation pattern is Zeta Reticuli. This is a double system with two yellow stars shining at magnitudes 5.2 and 5.5, and is just 39 light years from Earth. These two stars are thought to be very old and long-lived. They have a different composition to the Sun and may have shone steadily for 8 billion years already. This, along with their proximity, has made them a target for a forthcoming NASA telescope, which will look for signs of Earth-like planets.

α

ζ^1

β

Hydrus

This is another of Lacaille's eighteenth-century southern constellations from the group named after scientific instruments. Reticulum is a faint but distinct diamond shape consisting of four stars with a fifth in the middle, a little way to the southeast of the bright star Canopus in Carina. Reticulum is the Latin for 'net'. However, Lacaille meant his constellation to represent the crosshair, or reticle, which is inserted in a telescope eyepiece and used for accurately positioning stars in the middle of the field and measuring their precise position. There is no earlier mythology linked with this constellation.

Sagitta

Sagitta is Latin for arrow, interpreted by some as cupid's arrow or as the arrow shot at Scorpius by Sagittarius.

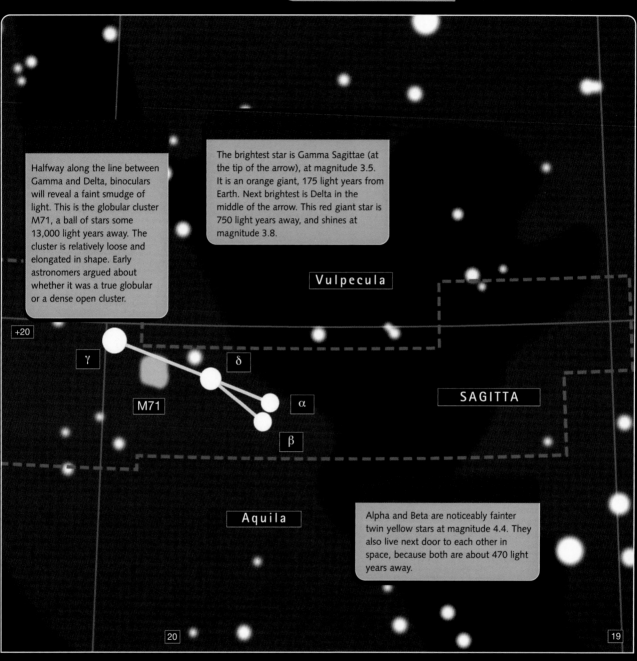

Halfway along the line between Gamma and Delta, binoculars will reveal a faint smudge of light. This is the globular cluster M71, a ball of stars some 13,000 light years away. The cluster is relatively loose and elongated in shape. Early astronomers argued about whether it was a true globular or a dense open cluster.

The brightest star is Gamma Sagittae (at the tip of the arrow), at magnitude 3.5. It is an orange giant, 175 light years from Earth. Next brightest is Delta in the middle of the arrow. This red giant star is 750 light years away, and shines at magnitude 3.8.

Vulpecula

+20

γ

δ

M71

α

SAGITTA

β

Aquila

Alpha and Beta are noticeably fainter twin yellow stars at magnitude 4.4. They also live next door to each other in space, because both are about 470 light years away.

20

19

Sagitta is a small but easily spotted constellation, representing an arrow. It lies due north of Aquila, and even though it is in the middle of the Milky Way, Sagitta has little of real interest within it. The constellation dates back to ancient Greek times, and according to one legend, it was believed to be the arrow that was shot by Hercules towards the Eagle (Aquila) and the Swan (Cygnus). Others saw it as an arrow fired by Cupid, or by Sagittarius at Scorpius. Still others interpreted the arrow as being shot by Centaurus at Aquila, as Centaurus faces the right direction and is in the correct position to fire it.

Sagittarius

Sagittarius is the Latin name for archer. The Greeks identified this archer as a centaur as he seemed to have a horse-like body.

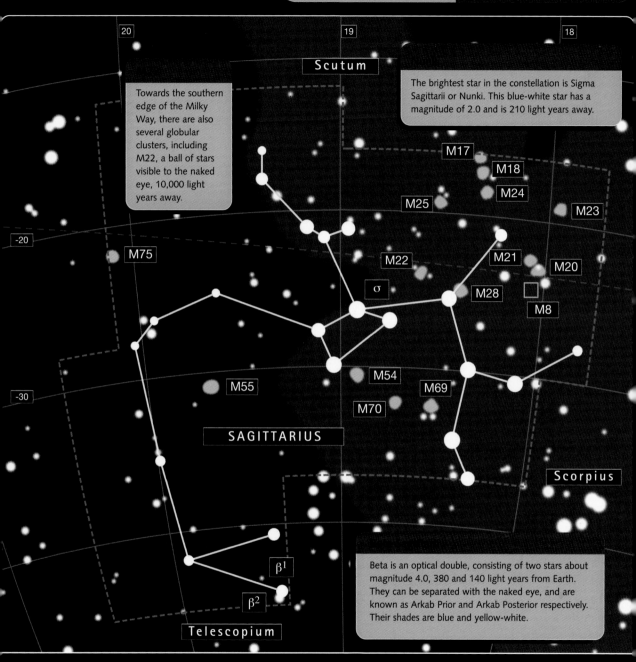

20 19 18

Scutum

Towards the southern edge of the Milky Way, there are also several globular clusters, including M22, a ball of stars visible to the naked eye, 10,000 light years away.

The brightest star in the constellation is Sigma Sagittarii or Nunki. This blue-white star has a magnitude of 2.0 and is 210 light years away.

M17

M18

M24

M25

M23

-20

M75

M22

M21

M20

σ

M28

M8

M54

M69

M55

M70

-30

SAGITTARIUS

Scorpius

β¹

β²

Beta is an optical double, consisting of two stars about magnitude 4.0, 380 and 140 light years from Earth. They can be separated with the naked eye, and are known as Arkab Prior and Arkab Posterior respectively. Their shades are blue and yellow-white.

Telescopium

The archer in this constellation is called Crotus. According to Greek mythology, he was the son of the Greek god and inventor of archery, Pan, and is usually depicted as a half-man, half-horse beast like Centaurus. A zodiac constellation, it is one of the most spectacular regions of the heavens, because it lies in the same direction as the middle of the Milky Way Galaxy. As a result, this is where the Milky Way star clouds are at their most dense. The real highlights of Sagittarius are its deep-sky objects. A number of nebulae and open star clusters lie in the northern half of the constellation.

Scorpius

Scorpius is the Latin name for scorpion. The scorpion of this constellation is the creature called up by Hera to kill the hunter Orion.

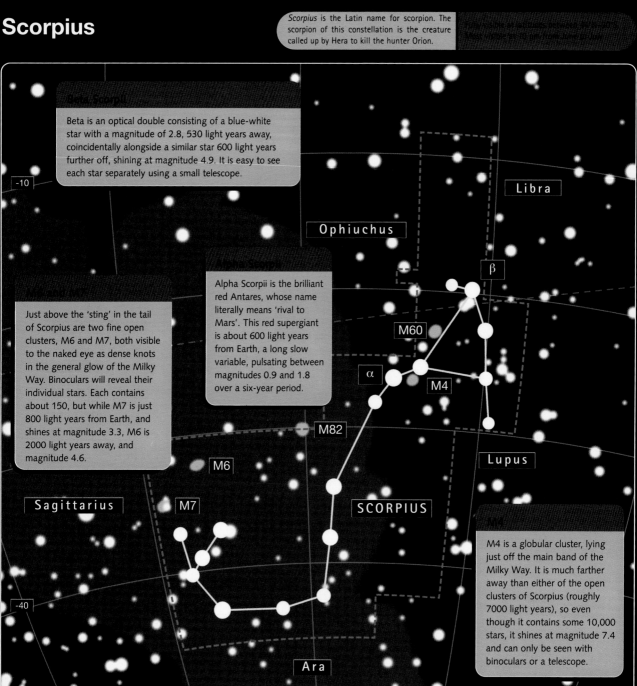

Beta Scorpii

Beta is an optical double consisting of a blue-white star with a magnitude of 2.8, 530 light years away, coincidentally alongside a similar star 600 light years further off, shining at magnitude 4.9. It is easy to see each star separately using a small telescope.

-10

Libra

Ophiuchus

β

Alpha Scorpii is the brilliant red Antares, whose name literally means 'rival to Mars'. This red supergiant is about 600 light years from Earth, a long slow variable, pulsating between magnitudes 0.9 and 1.8 over a six-year period.

M60

Just above the 'sting' in the tail of Scorpius are two fine open clusters, M6 and M7, both visible to the naked eye as dense knots in the general glow of the Milky Way. Binoculars will reveal their individual stars. Each contains about 150, but while M7 is just 800 light years from Earth, and shines at magnitude 3.3, M6 is 2000 light years away, and magnitude 4.6.

α

M4

M82

M6

Lupus

Sagittarius

M7

SCORPIUS

M4 is a globular cluster, lying just off the main band of the Milky Way. It is much farther away than either of the open clusters of Scorpius (roughly 7000 light years), so even though it contains some 10,000 stars, it shines at magnitude 7.4 and can only be seen with binoculars or a telescope.

-40

Ara

Scorpius, like Sagittarius just next door, is a spectacular constellation crossed by dense Milky Way star clouds. It is said to represent the Scorpion that killed the hunter Orion. However, even though Orion and the scorpion feature together in mythology, the constellation of Orion is almost opposite to Scorpius in the sky: this may have been a precautionary measure taken by the gods to prevent any further feuding between the two. In another story, Phaëton lost control of the chariot (see Eridanus) because his horses were frightened by the sight of the scorpion, tail raised to strike.

Sculptor

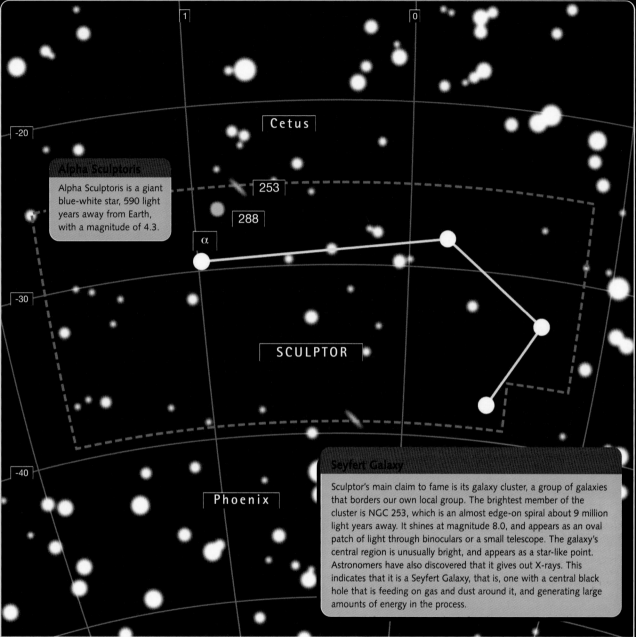

Cetus

Alpha Sculptoris

Alpha Sculptoris is a giant blue-white star, 590 light years away from Earth, with a magnitude of 4.3.

253

288

α

-20

-30

-40

SCULPTOR

Phoenix

Seyfert Galaxy

Sculptor's main claim to fame is its galaxy cluster, a group of galaxies that borders our own local group. The brightest member of the cluster is NGC 253, which is an almost edge-on spiral about 9 million light years away. It shines at magnitude 8.0, and appears as an oval patch of light through binoculars or a small telescope. The galaxy's central region is unusually bright, and appears as a star-like point. Astronomers have also discovered that it gives out X-rays. This indicates that it is a Seyfert Galaxy, that is, one with a central black hole that is feeding on gas and dust around it, and generating large amounts of energy in the process.

Sculptor is another small, faint and obscure constellation courtesy of Nicolas Louis de Lacaille, dreamt up by him during his survey to fill up holes in the southern sky in the 17th century. Bizarrely, it is supposed to represent a sculptor's workshop and was originally called Apparatus Sculptoris. (The name has since been shortened to Sculptor.) It's little wonder, in this case, that the four faint stars in the constellation pattern bear no relationship at all to the object they are supposed to represent. There is no earlier mythology associated with this constellation.

Scutum

R Scuti is another variable, and much easier to follow. It lies just to the south of Beta, and at its brightest almost matches it at magnitude 4.5. However, at its dimmest it drops to magnitude 8.8, only visible in a small telescope. The star is a yellow supergiant, and its light varies in a 144-day cycle. Astronomers still do not fully understand how it works.

Ophiuchus

β

R

M11

Aquila

M26

δ

-10

SCUTUM

Just to the south of R Scuti lies M11, a dense, rich, open cluster known as the Wild Duck. It contains 200 stars in a region of space half the size of the Full Moon, shining with an overall magnitude of around 5.5.

Delta Scuti is an unusual short-period variable that changes its brightness as it pulsates slightly, in a repeating cycle of just 4 hours and 40 minutes. However, its brightness only varies between magnitude 4.7 and 4.8, so it is almost impossible to detect with the naked eye.

-20

Sagittarius

20

19

18

This constellation is small and has faint stars in an indistinct pattern. Introduced in 1683 by Johannes Hevelius, it was originally called Scutum Sobieski (Sobieski's Shield). It is named after Hevelius's patron, the Polish king, John III Sobieski (1629–1696), in commemoration of the victory of the Christian forces under Sobieski's leadership at the Battle of Vienna in 1683. Hevelius inserted the constellation into a region of the Milky Way between Serpens Cauda and Aquila, where it remains today. It is now just called 'The Shield', and it is one of the few constellations named after an historical figure.

Serpens

Serpens is the Latin name for snake. *Serpens cauda* means tail of the snake and *serpens caput* means head of the snake.

18 17 16

Theta Serpentis, or Alya, marks the tip of the snake's tail. Small telescopes will show that it is binary, with twin white stars of magnitudes 4.6 and 5.0, about 100 light years away.

Alpha Serpentis (Unukalhai) is an orange giant, 70 light years away, and shines at magnitude 2.7.

+20

M5 in Serpens Caput is an impressive globular cluster of stars, visible on dark nights with the naked eye at magnitude 5.6. It is 24,500 light years away, and so larger telescopes are needed to separate its individual stars.

Hercules

SERPENS CAPUT

+10

Ophiuchus

α

M5

0

0

θ

SERPENS CAUDA

Libra

-10

M16 in Serpens Cauda is a distant open cluster, about 8000 light years from Earth, and visible through binoculars. It is embedded within the beautiful Eagle Nebula, home to the famous 'pillars of creation'. This is the name for the photograph taken by the Hubble Space Telescope, which shows towering dust clouds within which young stars are still forming.

M16

The constellation of Serpens is unique in that it is the only constellation that is split in two parts. It portrays a serpent curled around Ophiuchus (the serpent bearer) with Serpens Caput (the snake's head) held in Ophiuchus's left hand. Serpens Cauda (the snake's tail) continues to the east. The star

Alpha Serpentis is also known as Unukalhai, Arabic for 'serpent's neck'. Both Ophiuchus and Serpens were named by Ptolemy and their mythology is closely linked. This is the serpent from whom Asclepius, the physician, fatally learnt the secrets of life and death.

Sextans

Sextans is the Latin name for the sextant, a navigational device used for measuring the position of stars.

Fully visible at latitudes between 78° and 83°. Most visible at 10 pm from March to April.

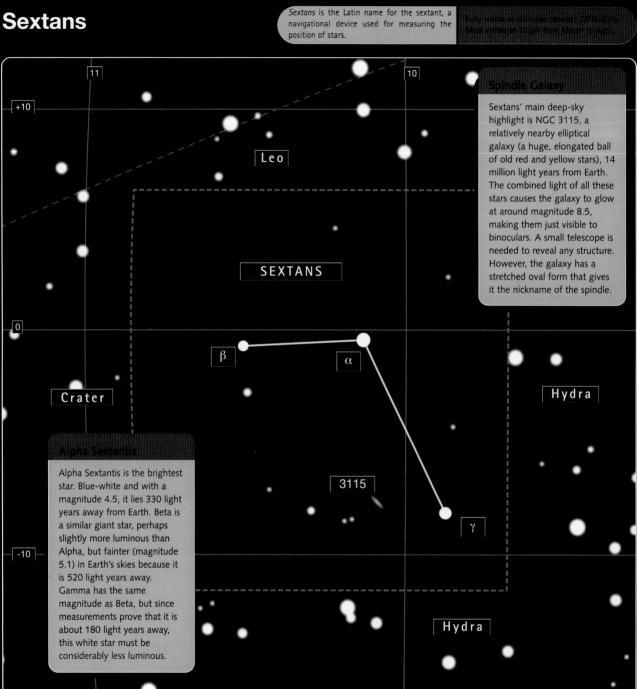

Spindle Galaxy

Sextans' main deep-sky highlight is NGC 3115, a relatively nearby elliptical galaxy (a huge, elongated ball of old red and yellow stars), 14 million light years from Earth. The combined light of all these stars causes the galaxy to glow at around magnitude 8.5, making them just visible to binoculars. A small telescope is needed to reveal any structure. However, the galaxy has a stretched oval form that gives it the nickname of the spindle.

Alpha Sextantis

Alpha Sextantis is the brightest star. Blue-white and with a magnitude 4.5, it lies 330 light years away from Earth. Beta is a similar giant star, perhaps slightly more luminous than Alpha, but fainter (magnitude 5.1) in Earth's skies because it is 520 light years away. Gamma has the same magnitude as Beta, but since measurements prove that it is about 180 light years away, this white star must be considerably less luminous.

While most of the constellations named after scientific instruments were inventions of Nicolas Louis de Lacaille, Sextans (the sextant) predates them. The Polish astronomer, Johannes Hevelius, added it to the sky in 1687. A sextant is an instrument for measuring the positions of objects in the sky, and Hevelius would have made regular use of one himself. The constellation itself is rather uninspiring. It consists of a handful of faint stars, all below magnitude 4. However, it is relatively easy to locate because it lies on the celestial equator, directly to the south of Leo.

Taurus

Taurus is the Latin name for bull. Here the bull may be the one that Zeus turned himself into to seduce Princess Europa.

Fully visible at latitudes between 88°N–58°S. Most visible at 10 pm December to January

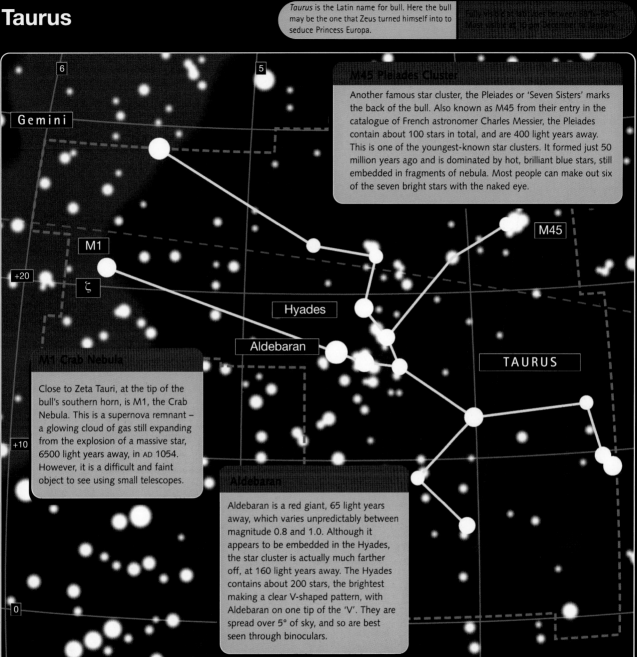

6

5

Gemini

M45 Pleiades Cluster

Another famous star cluster, the Pleiades or 'Seven Sisters' marks the back of the bull. Also known as M45 from their entry in the catalogue of French astronomer Charles Messier, the Pleiades contain about 100 stars in total, and are 400 light years away. This is one of the youngest-known star clusters. It formed just 50 million years ago and is dominated by hot, brilliant blue stars, still embedded in fragments of nebula. Most people can make out six of the seven bright stars with the naked eye.

M45

M1

+20

ζ

Hyades

Aldebaran

TAURUS

M1 Crab Nebula

Close to Zeta Tauri, at the tip of the bull's southern horn, is M1, the Crab Nebula. This is a supernova remnant – a glowing cloud of gas still expanding from the explosion of a massive star, 6500 light years away, in AD 1054. However, it is a difficult and faint object to see using small telescopes.

+10

Aldebaran

Aldebaran is a red giant, 65 light years away, which varies unpredictably between magnitude 0.8 and 1.0. Although it appears to be embedded in the Hyades, the star cluster is actually much farther off, at 160 light years away. The Hyades contains about 200 stars, the brightest making a clear V-shaped pattern, with Aldebaran on one tip of the 'V'. They are spread over 5° of sky, and so are best seen through binoculars.

0

This constellation is situated between Aries and Gemini. Taurus, the bull, is one of the oldest constellations, dating back to the earliest Babylonian astronomers. It may even be portrayed in the Great Hall of the Bulls in the 16,500-year-old cave paintings of Lascaux in southwestern France.

In Greek mythology this constellation represents the front half of the body of the bull that Zeus transformed himself into in order to abduct and seduce Princess Europa of Phoenicia. The bull's face is marked by the bright star Aldebaran, and an open star cluster called the Hyades.

Telescopium

Telescopium is Latin for telescope. This constellation was part of a group named in honour of scientific instruments by Lacaille.

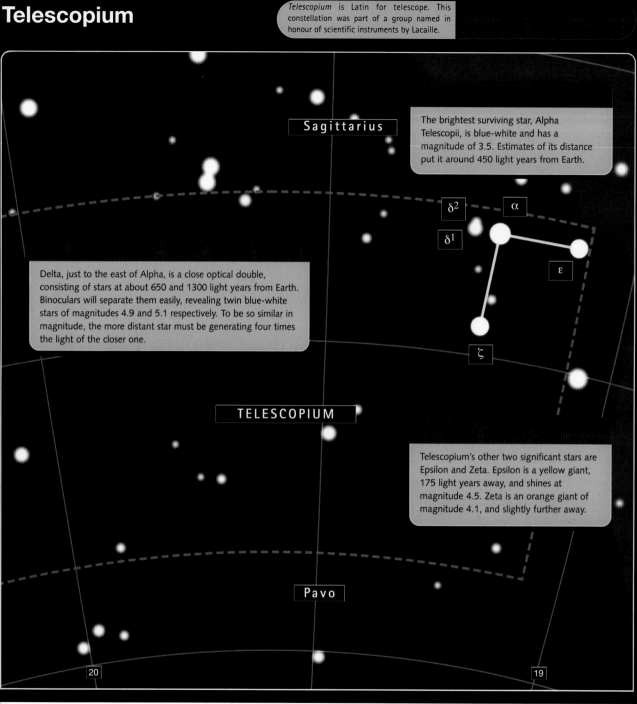

Sagittarius

The brightest surviving star, Alpha Telescopii, is blue-white and has a magnitude of 3.5. Estimates of its distance put it around 450 light years from Earth.

δ^2
δ^1
α
ε
ζ

Delta, just to the east of Alpha, is a close optical double, consisting of stars at about 650 and 1300 light years from Earth. Binoculars will separate them easily, revealing twin blue-white stars of magnitudes 4.9 and 5.1 respectively. To be so similar in magnitude, the more distant star must be generating four times the light of the closer one.

TELESCOPIUM

Telescopium's other two significant stars are Epsilon and Zeta. Epsilon is a yellow giant, 175 light years away, and shines at magnitude 4.5. Zeta is an orange giant of magnitude 4.1, and slightly further away.

Pavo

20

19

This constellation, supposed to represent a telescope, is among the worst offenders for contrived constellations. Nicolas Louis de Lacaille seems to have simply encircled a rectangular region of the southern sky containing a few faint stars. Even the supposed 'asterism' sits awkwardly in the northwest corner. The awkward shape of the constellation today is really due to Lacaille's audacity. To make a convincing constellation, he 'stole' significant stars from nearby constellations. These were returned to their rightful owners in 1929, but this left Telescopium even more barren.

Triangulum

Triangulum, as its name suggests, forms a right triangle. The ancient Greeks saw it as the letter delta, others thought it was the island of Sicily.

Andromeda

The brightest star is Beta Trianguli, a white giant of magnitude 3.0, 135 light years from Earth. By comparison, Alpha, although also white and less than half the distance of Beta, is fainter at magnitude 3.4. According to our understanding of how stars burn, Beta must be more massive than Alpha to explain the brightness difference.

β

TRIANGULUM

M33

α

Aries

Pisces

While Triangulum's stars are unremarkable, it has one outstanding object – the Triangulum Galaxy M33. This spiral is the third major member of the Local Group of galaxies (after the Milky Way and Andromeda). It is slightly more distant than Andromeda, at about 2.8 million light years, and is face-on to us, so we see its spiral arms clearly. However because the galaxy's light is more widely spread out, covering an area of sky larger than the Full Moon, it appears very faint, and can only be spotted using binoculars or a small telescope.

The small constellation of Triangulum is compact but distinct, consisting of three stars of moderate brightness forming a wedge shape, between Perseus and the Square of Pegasus. It appears to point at Aries. The constellation dates back to ancient times and according to one story it was placed in the sky by Apollo as a pointer towards the more faint ram. It was also seen as a celestial version of the Greek letter, Delta. For a time it was called Triangulum Major (the Greater Triangle) after the Polish astronomer Hevelius invented a new, smaller triangle (Triangulum Minor) just to the south of it.

Triangulum Australe

Triangulum Australe is the Latin name for Southern Triangle. It was introduced in 1603 by Johannes Bayer.

Fully visible at latitudes between 19°N and 90°S. Most visible at 9pm during July.

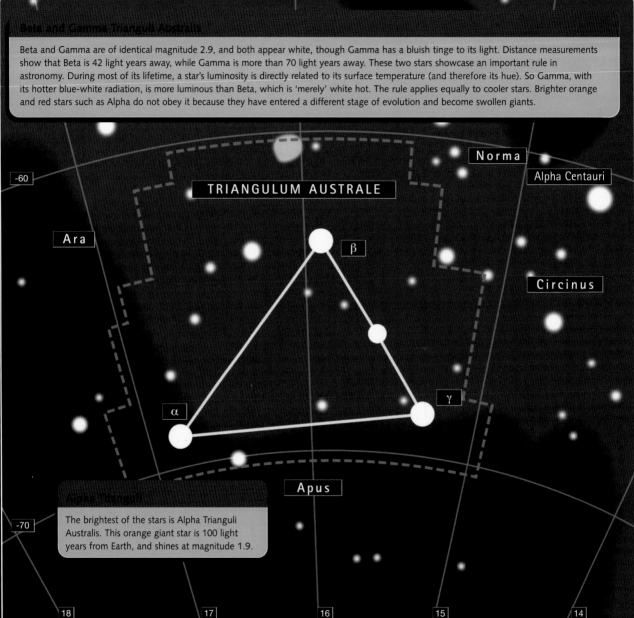

Beta and Gamma Trianguli Australis

Beta and Gamma are of identical magnitude 2.9, and both appear white, though Gamma has a bluish tinge to its light. Distance measurements show that Beta is 42 light years away, while Gamma is more than 70 light years away. These two stars showcase an important rule in astronomy. During most of its lifetime, a star's luminosity is directly related to its surface temperature (and therefore its hue). So Gamma, with its hotter blue-white radiation, is more luminous than Beta, which is 'merely' white hot. The rule applies equally to cooler stars. Brighter orange and red stars such as Alpha do not obey it because they have entered a different stage of evolution and become swollen giants.

Norma

Alpha Centauri

-60

TRIANGULUM AUSTRALE

Ara

β

Circinus

γ

α

Apus

Alpha Trianguli

-70

The brightest of the stars is Alpha Trianguli Australis. This orange giant star is 100 light years from Earth, and shines at magnitude 1.9.

18   17   16   15   14

The southern triangle is one of the few 'modern' constellations that resembles its name. A roughly equal-sided triangle of relatively bright stars, it lies directly to the southeast of Alpha Centauri. Johannes Bayer first records this easily spotted pattern in 1603, but there is a difference of opinion over the 'inventor'. It may have been the Dutch explorers Pieter Dirkszoon Keyser and Frederick de Houtman in the 1590s, or Dutch astronomer Petrus Theodorus Embdanus some decades earlier. There is also evidence that it could have been independently named by Arab astronomers.

Tucana

Tucana is the Latin name for the toucan, a brilliantly coloured, fruit-eating bird of tropical America, with a large, thin-walled beak.

Fully visible at latitudes between 14°N–90°S
Best visible at 10 pm September to November.

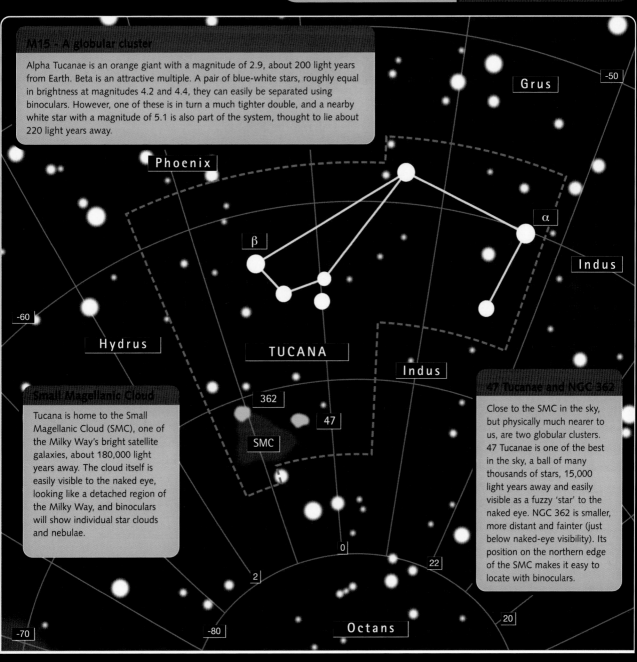

M15 – A globular cluster

Alpha Tucanae is an orange giant with a magnitude of 2.9, about 200 light years from Earth. Beta is an attractive multiple. A pair of blue-white stars, roughly equal in brightness at magnitudes 4.2 and 4.4, they can easily be separated using binoculars. However, one of these is in turn a much tighter double, and a nearby white star with a magnitude of 5.1 is also part of the system, thought to lie about 220 light years away.

Small Magellanic Cloud

Tucana is home to the Small Magellanic Cloud (SMC), one of the Milky Way's bright satellite galaxies, about 180,000 light years away. The cloud itself is easily visible to the naked eye, looking like a detached region of the Milky Way, and binoculars will show individual star clouds and nebulae.

47 Tucanae and NGC 362

Close to the SMC in the sky, but physically much nearer to us, are two globular clusters. 47 Tucanae is one of the best in the sky, a ball of many thousands of stars, 15,000 light years away and easily visible as a fuzzy 'star' to the naked eye. NGC 362 is smaller, more distant and fainter (just below naked-eye visibility). Its position on the northern edge of the SMC makes it easy to locate with binoculars.

Tucana, the Toucan, is another of the birds introduced to southern skies by Dutch navigators Pieter Dirkszoon Keyser and Frederick de Houtman in the late 16th century, and immortalized by Bayer in his star atlas *Uranometria* of 1603. It is situated close to the south pole of the sky, just to the west of Achernar, the bright star at the end of Eridanus. While its stars are generally faint and its pattern difficult to make out, the constellation is redeemed by a collection of fascinating deep-sky objects. It was invented in the 17th century, therefore there is no earlier mythology associated with Tucana.

Ursa Major

Ursa Major is the Latin name for Great Bear. Many different civilizations have seen this constellation as a bear.

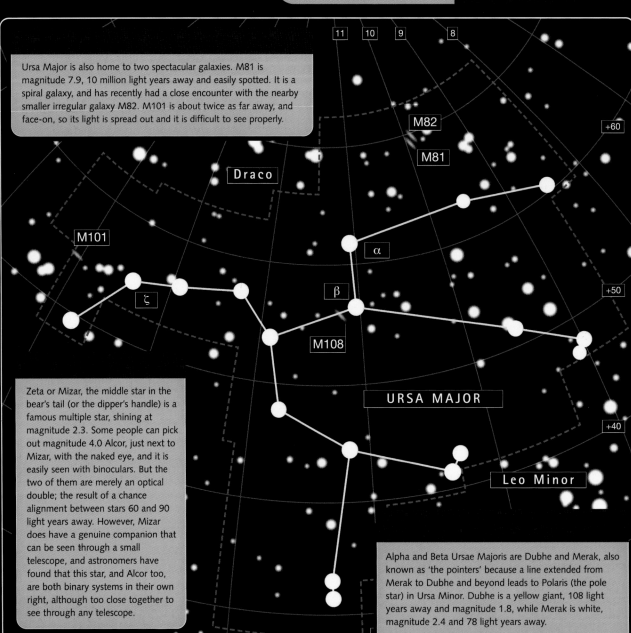

Ursa Major is also home to two spectacular galaxies. M81 is magnitude 7.9, 10 million light years away and easily spotted. It is a spiral galaxy, and has recently had a close encounter with the nearby smaller irregular galaxy M82. M101 is about twice as far away, and face-on, so its light is spread out and it is difficult to see properly.

Draco

M82

M81

+60

M101

α

β

+50

ζ

M108

URSA MAJOR

+40

Leo Minor

Zeta or Mizar, the middle star in the bear's tail (or the dipper's handle) is a famous multiple star, shining at magnitude 2.3. Some people can pick out magnitude 4.0 Alcor, just next to Mizar, with the naked eye, and it is easily seen with binoculars. But the two of them are merely an optical double; the result of a chance alignment between stars 60 and 90 light years away. However, Mizar does have a genuine companion that can be seen through a small telescope, and astronomers have found that this star, and Alcor too, are both binary systems in their own right, although too close together to see through any telescope.

Alpha and Beta Ursae Majoris are Dubhe and Merak, also known as 'the pointers' because a line extended from Merak to Dubhe and beyond leads to Polaris (the pole star) in Ursa Minor. Dubhe is a yellow giant, 108 light years away and magnitude 1.8, while Merak is white, magnitude 2.4 and 78 light years away.

One of the most famous constellations in the sky, Ursa Major (the Great Bear) is the third-largest in the sky, and is circumpolar so it never sets in the northern hemisphere. Ursa Major stretches well beyond the seven bright stars at its core. These core stars alone form a pattern known variously as the Plough or the Big Dipper. According to the Greek mythology, the bear here is Callisto, the daughter of Lycaon, king of Arcadia. Callisto was a hunting partner of Artemis, but she was seduced by Zeus (disguised as Apollo) and either Zeus's outraged wife, Hera, or Artemis turned Callisto into a bear.

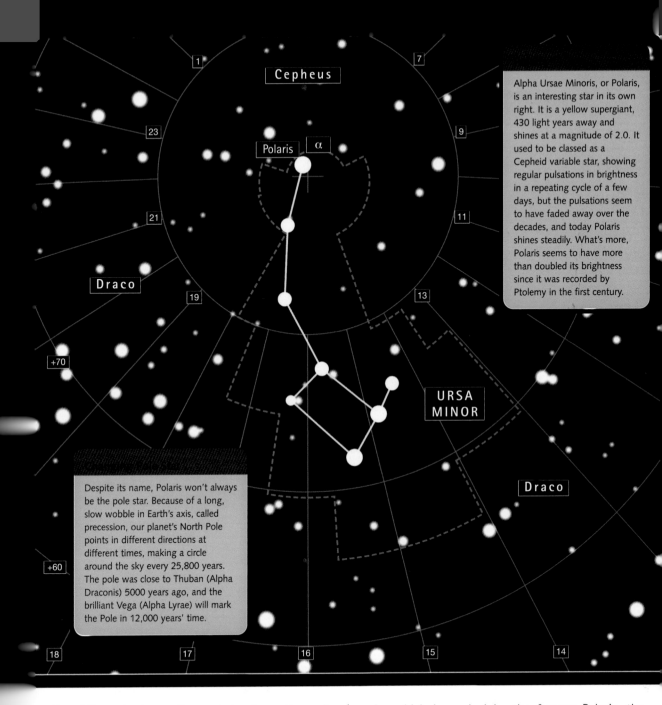

Cepheus

1 7

23 9

Polaris α

21 11

Draco

19 13

+70

URSA
MINOR

Draco

+60

18 17 16 15 14

Alpha Ursae Minoris, or Polaris, is an interesting star in its own right. It is a yellow supergiant, 430 light years away and shines at a magnitude of 2.0. It used to be classed as a Cepheid variable star, showing regular pulsations in brightness in a repeating cycle of a few days, but the pulsations seem to have faded away over the decades, and today Polaris shines steadily. What's more, Polaris seems to have more than doubled its brightness since it was recorded by Ptolemy in the first century.

Despite its name, Polaris won't always be the pole star. Because of a long, slow wobble in Earth's axis, called precession, our planet's North Pole points in different directions at different times, making a circle around the sky every 25,800 years. The pole was close to Thuban (Alpha Draconis) 5000 years ago, and the brilliant Vega (Alpha Lyrae) will mark the Pole in 12,000 years' time.

Ursa Minor, the Lesser Bear, mimics the pattern of the bright stars in the Big Dipper part of Ursa Major, with a fainter pattern of a rough rectangle attached to a 'tail' of three stars. This pattern is known as the Little Dipper. Ursa Minor stretches out from the North Celestial Pole, the pivot-point of the northern sky, which is marked by the famous Polaris, the constellation's brightest star. It is circumpolar, remaining visible all night throughout the year for almost the entire northern hemisphere. According to some legends, the tail of the Ursa Minor is very long because of its nonstop spinning round the pole.

Vela

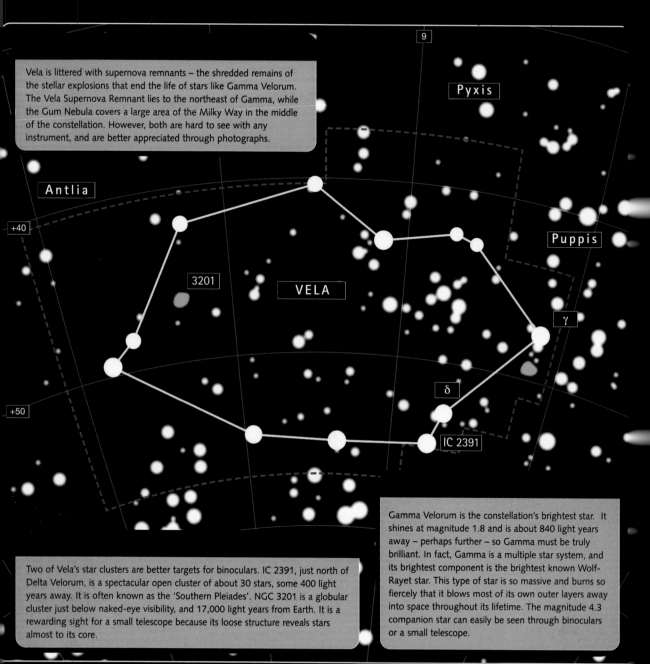

Vela is littered with supernova remnants – the shredded remains of the stellar explosions that end the life of stars like Gamma Velorum. The Vela Supernova Remnant lies to the northeast of Gamma, while the Gum Nebula covers a large area of the Milky Way in the middle of the constellation. However, both are hard to see with any instrument, and are better appreciated through photographs.

Pyxis

Antlia

+40

3201

VELA

Puppis

γ

δ

+50

IC 2391

Gamma Velorum is the constellation's brightest star. It shines at magnitude 1.8 and is about 840 light years away – perhaps further – so Gamma must be truly brilliant. In fact, Gamma is a multiple star system, and its brightest component is the brightest known Wolf-Rayet star. This type of star is so massive and burns so fiercely that it blows most of its own outer layers away into space throughout its lifetime. The magnitude 4.3 companion star can easily be seen through binoculars or a small telescope.

Two of Vela's star clusters are better targets for binoculars. IC 2391, just north of Delta Velorum, is a spectacular open cluster of about 30 stars, some 400 light years away. It is often known as the 'Southern Pleiades'. NGC 3201 is a globular cluster just below naked-eye visibility, and 17,000 light years from Earth. It is a rewarding sight for a small telescope because its loose structure reveals stars almost to its core.

This large southern constellation is one of the four parts into which the original, much larger constellation Argo Navis was split. Vela represents the sail of the *Argo*, the ship of the Greek mythological hero, Jason. Vela was once part of the even bigger constellation Argo Navis. It lies across a rich section of the southern Milky Way with Carina, Puppis and Pyxis, the other parts of the ship, and has an abundance of deep-sky objects, although many of these are beyond the range of amateur astronomers. Having been once part of Argo Navis, Vela has no other mythology associated with it.

Virgo

Virgo is the Latin term for virgin, although it is not clear who the constellation is meant to represent.

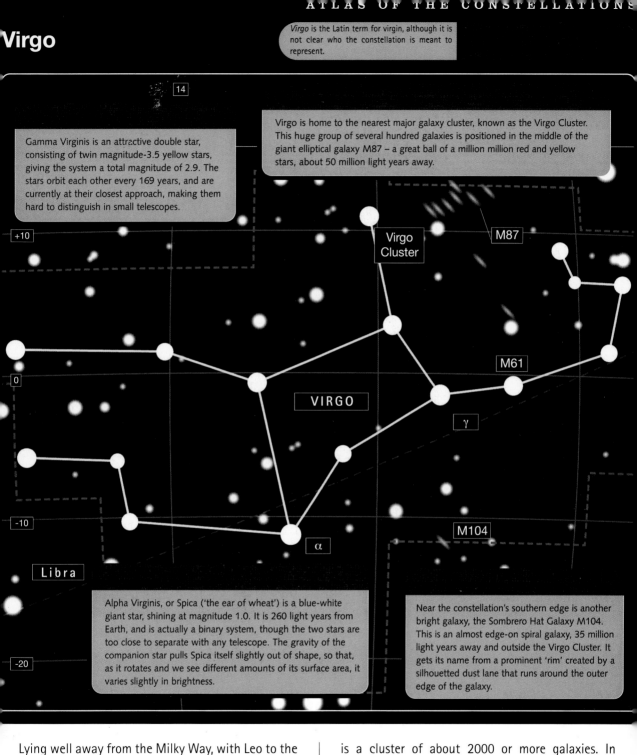

14

Gamma Virginis is an attractive double star, consisting of twin magnitude-3.5 yellow stars, giving the system a total magnitude of 2.9. The stars orbit each other every 169 years, and are currently at their closest approach, making them hard to distinguish in small telescopes.

Virgo is home to the nearest major galaxy cluster, known as the Virgo Cluster. This huge group of several hundred galaxies is positioned in the middle of the giant elliptical galaxy M87 – a great ball of a million million red and yellow stars, about 50 million light years away.

+10

Virgo Cluster

M87

0

VIRGO

M61

γ

-10

M104

Libra

α

Alpha Virginis, or Spica ('the ear of wheat') is a blue-white giant star, shining at magnitude 1.0. It is 260 light years from Earth, and is actually a binary system, though the two stars are too close to separate with any telescope. The gravity of the companion star pulls Spica itself slightly out of shape, so that, as it rotates and we see different amounts of its surface area, it varies slightly in brightness.

Near the constellation's southern edge is another bright galaxy, the Sombrero Hat Galaxy M104. This is an almost edge-on spiral galaxy, 35 million light years away and outside the Virgo Cluster. It gets its name from a prominent 'rim' created by a silhouetted dust lane that runs around the outer edge of the galaxy.

-20

Lying well away from the Milky Way, with Leo to the west and Libra to the east, this is the second-largest constellation in the sky. It is situated on the celestial equator and is one of the zodiac constellations. Its main attractions are an array of different galaxies, including the Virgo Cluster, which is a cluster of about 2000 or more galaxies. In mythology, the constellation is often seen as Astraea, the daughter of Zeus and Themis. Astraea was the Greek goddess of justice, which is why she holds the scales of justice. The virgin is also depicted as the Greek harvest goddess, Demeter.

Volans

Volans translates from the Latin as the flying fish, which the constellation's inventors encountered on their travels.

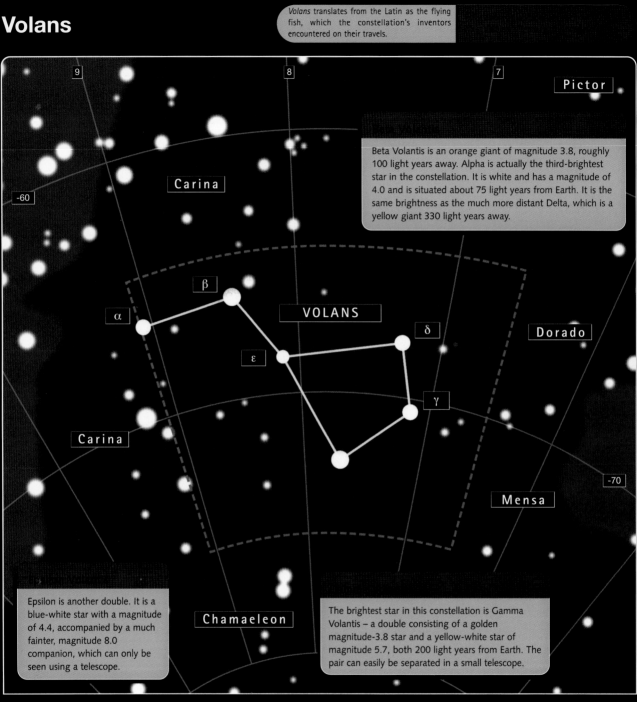

Pictor

Carina

-60

Beta Volantis is an orange giant of magnitude 3.8, roughly 100 light years away. Alpha is actually the third-brightest star in the constellation. It is white and has a magnitude of 4.0 and is situated about 75 light years from Earth. It is the same brightness as the much more distant Delta, which is a yellow giant 330 light years away.

β

α

VOLANS

δ

Dorado

ε

γ

Carina

-70

Mensa

Epsilon is another double. It is a blue-white star with a magnitude of 4.4, accompanied by a much fainter, magnitude 8.0 companion, which can only be seen using a telescope.

Chamaeleon

The brightest star in this constellation is Gamma Volantis – a double consisting of a golden magnitude-3.8 star and a yellow-white star of magnitude 5.7, both 200 light years from Earth. The pair can easily be separated in a small telescope.

Volans is another faint constellation, which lies next to Carina and was one of a dozen invented by the Dutch navigators Pieter Dirkszoon Keyser and Frederick de Houtman in the late 16th century. Most of their constellations were named after different birds, but in this case, Volans is named for the bizarre 'flying fish' that they encountered on their journeys and in the constellation it is depicted with its wing-like fins outspread as it glides over the waves. The constellation's pattern is indistinct, but it is easily located because it lies between the bright stars of Carina and the South Celestial Pole.

Vulpecula

Vulpecula translates from the Latin as little fox but the constellation is more commonly known simply as fox.

20

Cygnus

+30

M27 – Planetary Nebula

M27 is the constellation's best deep-sky object, the brightest and most easily seen planetary nebula in the sky. It lies about 1000 light years away, and is a glowing shell of gas, flung off by a dying star that has since faded to magnitude 13, and now covering about one-eighth of a degree in the sky (one-quarter the diameter of the Full Moon). It is best seen through binoculars or a telescope on low magnification, to make the most of its contrast with the background sky.

Alpha Vulpecula

Alpha Vulpeculae, the brightest star in the constellation, is a red giant about 250 light years away, which shines at magnitude 4.4.

α

VULPECULA

PSR 1919+21

M27

+20

Brocchi's Cluster

PSR 1919+21 is the remains of another dead star, although this one died in a much more spectacular fashion as a supernova. It has left behind a pulsar, a rapidly spinning, incredibly dense neutron star whose magnetic field channels its radiation into two lighthouse-like beams that sweep across space as the star rotates. The end result is a star that apparently blinks on and off every 1.3 seconds. The Vulpecula pulsar was the first to be discovered, in 1967, and, at first, the astronomers who found it wondered if they had found a signal from an alien civilization.

Aquila

Lying just to the west of Pegasus and southeast of Lyra, the constellation Vulpecula, the fox, is one of a handful of additions to the northern sky made by Polish astronomer Johannes Hevelius in his book, *Uranographia*, published in 1690. Its stars are faint and have no obvious pattern. On Vulpecula's southern border lies Brocchi's Cluster, a small but attractive group of stars around the limit of naked-eye visibility, and an attractive target for binoculars. The constellation was first known as *Vulpecula cum ansere*, meaning the fox with the goose. The goose, which was in the fox's jaws, in no longer in the sky.

Star Charts

There are many ways to divide up the night sky. These charts use one of the simplest, splitting it into six segments of roughly equal extent: four along the celestial equator, and one each for the poles. The chart on this page shows the night sky around the north celestial pole.

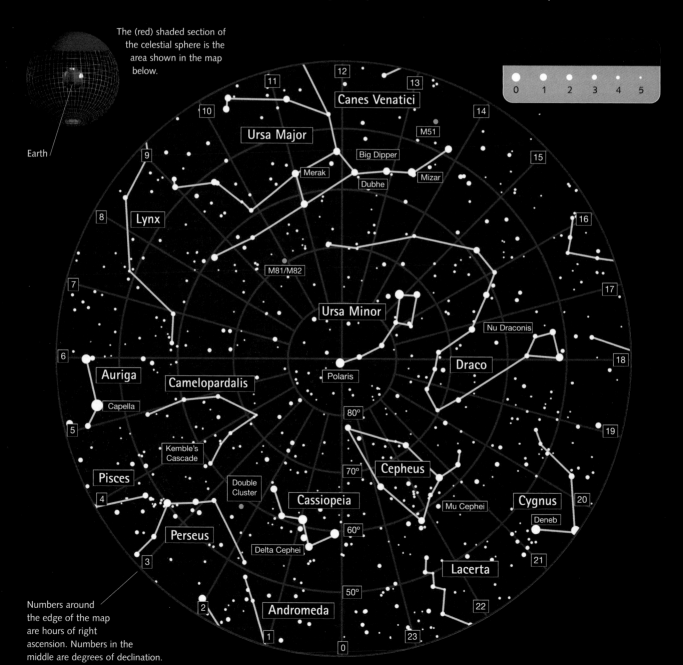

The (red) shaded section of the celestial sphere is the area shown in the map below.

Earth

0 1 2 3 4 5

11
12
13
10
Canes Venatici
14
Ursa Major
M51
9
Big Dipper
15
Merak
Dubhe
Mizar
8
Lynx
16
M81/M82
7
Ursa Minor
Nu Draconis
17
6
Draco
18
Auriga
Camelopardalis
Polaris
Capella
80°
5
19
Kemble's Cascade
70°
Cepheus
Pisces
Double Cluster
4
Cassiopeia
Mu Cephei
Cygnus
20
Delta Cephei
60°
Deneb
Perseus
3
Lacerta
21
2
50°
22
Andromeda
1
0
23

Numbers around the edge of the map are hours of right ascension. Numbers in the middle are degrees of declination.

The Night Sky Around the Square of Pegasus

The (red) shaded section, detailed in the map below, is usually visible in the night sky from September to December.

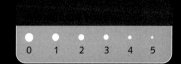

0   1   2   3   4   5

Numbers along the bottom edge of the map are hours of right ascension. Numbers along the left edge are degrees of declination.

M39

Cassiopeia

Cygnus

NGC 891

40°

Andromeda

M31

Lacerta

Triangulum

Gamma
Andromedae

Alpheratz

Scheatz

30°

M33

Aries

Hamal

Square
of
Pegasus

Pegasus

20°

Markab

M15

Algenib

Piscis

Equuleus

M2

0°

Aquarius

Mira

Cetus

-10

Helix Nebula

-20

Diphda

Formalhaut

NGC 253

Fornax

Piscis Austrinus

-30

Sculptor

NGC 55

Eridanus

Phoenix

-40

Grus

2

1

0

23

22

The Night Sky Around Orion

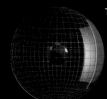

This (red) section shows Orion with some of the most famous constellations and is rich in bright star clusters, including Sirius – the brightest star in the night sky.

Magnitude scale
0 1 2 3 4 5

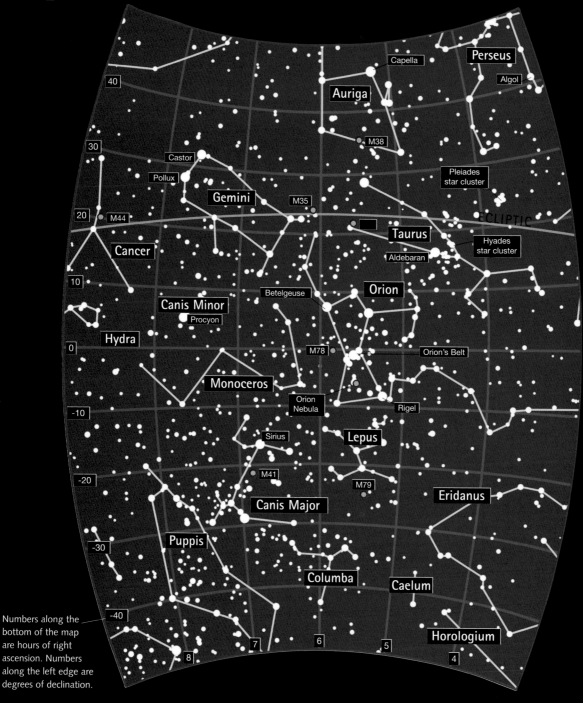

Numbers along the bottom of the map are hours of right ascension. Numbers along the left edge are degrees of declination.

The Night Sky Around Ursa Major

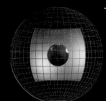

This map covers the area of the night sky in the 12 hour region of right ascension. It is home to several galaxies which spill over from Leo and Virgo into Coma Berenices and surrounding constellations.

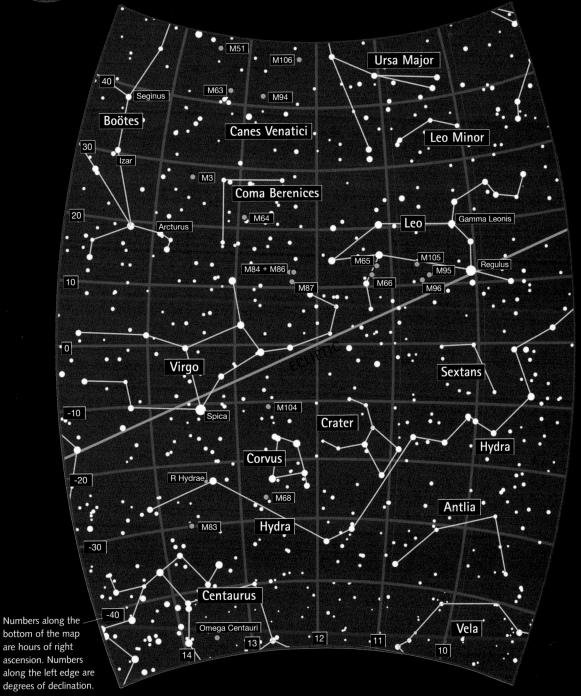

Numbers along the bottom of the map are hours of right ascension. Numbers along the left edge are degrees of declination.

The Night Sky Around the Milky Way

This map covers the area of the night sky in the 18 hour region of right ascension. The brightest part of the Milky Way is clearly visible between June and August around Scorpius and Scutum.

Numbers along the bottom of the map are hours of right ascension. Numbers along the left edge are degrees of declination.

The Southern Polar Night Sky

The stars and constellations in this area of the night sky are always visible (at certain times) from the southern hemisphere. Although there is no bright star very close to the pole, there are several between -40° and -60° such as Alpha Centauri and Canopus.

Numbers around the edge of the map are hours of right ascension. Numbers in the middle are degrees of declination.

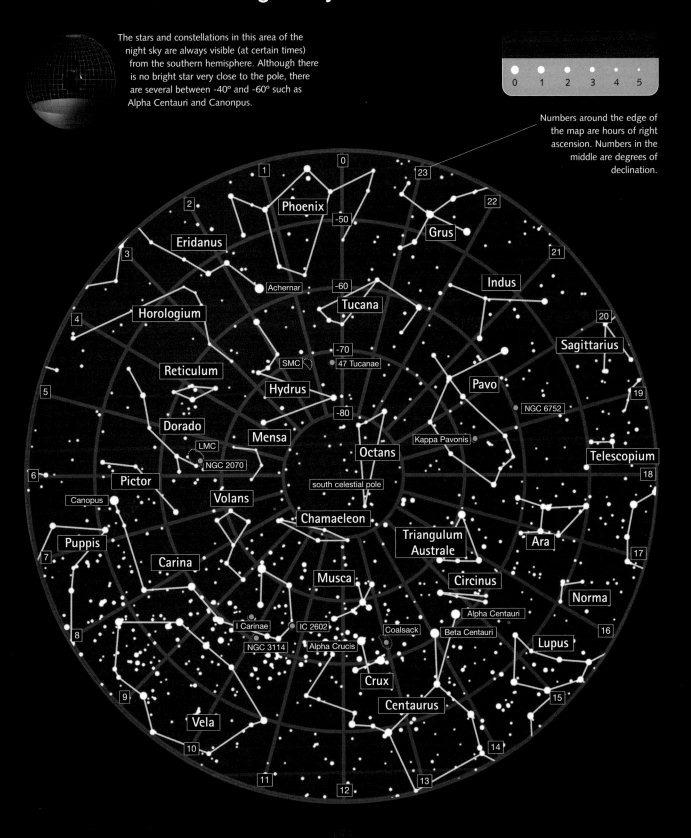

0 1 2 3 4 5

Phoenix
Eridanus
Grus
Indus
Horologium
Achernar
-50
Tucana
-60
Sagittarius
Reticulum
SMC
-70
47 Tucanae
Pavo
20
Hydrus
-80
NGC 6752
Dorado
Mensa
Octans
Kappa Pavonis
Telescopium
LMC
NGC 2070
south celestial pole
Pictor
Canopus
Volans
Chamaeleon
18
Puppis
Triangulum Australe
Ara
Carina
Musca
Circinus
Norma
I Carinae
IC 2602
Alpha Centauri
NGC 3114
Alpha Crucis
Coalsack
Beta Centauri
Lupus
Crux
Centaurus
Vela
15

Table of Constellations

This table lists all the constellations with their English translation and the date they were first documented. We also list the constellation's name in genitive case. This Latin form denotes belonging, and is used in astronomy when describing a specific star. For example the brightest star in Centaurus is Alpha Centauri.

Andromeda	Andromedae	Princess Andromeda	ancient
Antlia	Antliae	Vacuum pump	1763
Apus	Apodis	Bird of paradise	1603
Aquarius	Aquarii	Waterbearer	ancient
Aquila	Aquilae	Eagle	ancient
Ara	Arae	Altar	ancient
Aries	Arietis	Ram	ancient
Auriga	Aurigae	Charioteer	ancient
Boötes	Boötis	Herder	ancient
Caelum	Caeli	Engraving tool	1763
Camelopardalis	Camelopardalis	Giraffe	1613
Cancer	Cancri	Crab	ancient
Canes Venatici	Canum Venaticorum	Hunting dogs	1687
Canis Major	Canis Majoris	Greater dog	ancient
Canis Minor	Canis Minoris	Lesser dog	ancient
Capricornus	Capricorni	Horned like a goat	ancient
Carina	Carinae	Keel	1763
Cassiopeia	Cassiopeiae	An Ethiopian queen	ancient
Centaurus	Centauri	Centaur	ancient
Cepheus	Cephei	An Ethiopian king	ancient
Cetus	Ceti	Whale	ancient
Chamaeleon	Chamaeleontis	Chameleon	1603
Circinus	Circini	Dividing compasses	1763
Columba	Columbae	Dove	1592
Coma Berenices	Comae Berenices	Berenice's hair	1603
Corona Australis	Coronae Australis	Southern crown	ancient
Corona Borealis	Coronae Borealis	Northern crown	ancient
Corvus	Corvi	Raven or crow	ancient
Crater	Crateris	Cup or chalice	ancient
Crux	Crucis	Cross	1603
Cygnus	Cygni	Swan	ancient
Delphinus	Delphini	Dolphin	ancient
Dorado	Doradus	Dolphinfish	1603
Draco	Draconis	Dragon	ancient
Equuleus	Equulei	Little horse	ancient
Eridanus	Eridani	River Eridanus	ancient
Fornax	Fornacis	Furnace	1763
Gemini	Geminorum	Twins	ancient
Grus	Gruis	Crane	1603
Hercules	Herculis	Hercules	ancient
Horologium	Horologii	Clock	1763

Hydra	Hydrae	Water snake	ancient
Hydrus	Hydri	Male water snake	1603
Indus	Indi	Native American	1603
Lacerta	Lacertae	Lizard	1690
Leo	Leonis	Lion	ancient
Leo Minor	Leonis Minoris	Lesser lion	1690
Lepus	Leporis	Hare	ancient
Libra	Librae	Scales	ancient
Lupus	Lupi	Wolf	ancient
Lynx	Lyncis	Lynx	1690
Lyra	Lyrae	Lyre	ancient
Mensa	Mensae	Table	1763
Microscopium	Microscopii	Microscope	1763
Monoceros	Monocerotis	Unicorn	1624
Musca	Muscae	Fly	1603
Norma	Normae	Normal (right angle)	1763
Octans	Octantis	Octant	1763
Ophiuchus	Ophiuchi	Asclepius	ancient
Orion	Orionis	Orion, son of Poseidon	ancient
Pavo	Pavonis	Peacock	1603
Pegasus	Pegasi	Pegasus	ancient
Perseus	Persei	Perseus	ancient
Phoenix	Phoenicis	Phoenix	1603
Pictor	Pictoris	Painter's easel	1763
Pisces	Piscium	Fish	ancient
Piscis Austrinus	Piscis Austrini	Southern fish	ancient
Puppis	Puppis	Poop deck	1763
Pyxis	Pyxidis	Compass	1763
Reticulum	Reticuli	Grid or reticule	1763
Sagitta	Sagittae	Arrow	ancient
Sagittarius	Sagittarii	Archer	ancient
Scorpius	Scorpii	Scorpion	ancient
Sculptor	Sculptoris	Sculptor's studio	1763
Scutum	Scuti	Shield	1690
Serpens	Serpentis	Snake	ancient
Sextans	Sextantis	Sextant	1690
Taurus	Tauri	Bull	ancient
Telescopium	Telescopii	Telescope	1763
Triangulum	Trianguli	Right triangle	ancient
Triangulum Australe	Trianguli Australis	Southern Triangle	1603
Tucana	Tucanae	Toucan	1603
Ursa Major	Ursae Majoris	Great bear	ancient
Ursa Minor	Ursae Minoris	Lesser bear	ancient
Vela	Velorum	Sails	1763
Virgo	Virginis	Virgin	ancient
Volans	Volantis	Flying fish	1603
Vulpecula	Vulpeculae	Little fox	1690

Index